Reader's Digest

READING skill BUilDER™

ADVANCED

PROJECT EDITOR: **WARREN J. HALLIBURTON**

EDITOR: **JUDITH PIERSON**

CONSULTANTS:

Jorge Garcia, Ed. D.
Supervisor Secondary Reading
Hillsborough County Public
Schools
Tampa, Florida

Susan Pasquini
Reading Specialist /
English Instructor
Escondido High School
San Diego, California

Frank Vernol
Instructional Learning
Secondary Reading
Dallas Independent School
District
Dallas, Texas

Grace Whittaker
Secondary Reading Supervisor
Boston Public Schools
Boston, Massachusetts

READER'S DIGEST EDUCATIONAL DIVISION
The credits and acknowledgments that appear on the inside
back cover are hereby made a part of this copyright page.

Reader's Digest ® Trademark Reg. U.S. Pat. Off. Marca Registrada ISBN 0-88300-273-5

□□□ □□□ □ Part 2

Reorder No. B23

CONTENTS

Roller Coaster: King of the Park · *Robert Cartmell*
4

He Dives After Treasure · *Stephen C. Michaud*
30

Doctor for the People · *Elizabeth Levy and Mara Miller*
16

Tung Is My Name · *Tseng Pei-yao*
40

A Home In Space · *The Editors of Boys' Life*
24

White-Water High · *Jean George*
46

Stories for which Audio Lessons are available.

A Spanish Ghost Story ·
*Ralph S. Boggs and Mary G.
Davis*
54

Burning Up the Links · *Grace
Lichtenstein*
83

Magnificent Marathon ·
Sheila Cragg
63

**Down a Dark Hall at
Breakneck Speed** · *Sam
Posey*
100

Trouble At Churchill · *Richard
C. Davids*
73

Exploring the Unexplained ·
*Frank Edwards, David
Wallachinsky and Irving
Wallace*
112

Roller Coaster:

King of the Park

Robert Cartmell

Passengers
enjoying thrills
aboard somersaulting
roller coaster

There's a powerfully loud blast. Suddenly, your neck snaps back, and your stomach feels torn from its moorings. Loud screams, and more, and you are crash-speeding up a steep incline. At the top, you pause—just long enough to catch your breath and get a good view of the land (if you dare open your eyes). You drop almost straight down 75 feet (23 meters). The ground swerves and flips into the sky. More screaming, another somersault and then quiet.

Open your eyes. You have just finished riding in one of the hundreds of new "scream machines" drawing record crowds to amusement parks all over the country.

Recently, a Soviet track team was eager to ride the Rebel Yell at Kings Dominion, a theme park outside Richmond, Virginia. Though they did not speak English, the team kept chanting "Russian Mountains" during their ride. Later, their guide explained that roller coasters started out as ice slides built on a solid framework of wood in St. Petersburg, Russia, during the 17th century. Passengers sat in a guide's lap—both dangerously balanced on a 2-foot (0.6-meter) sled. They then shot down a 70-

foot (21-meter) high, 50-degree slope at dizzying speeds. The ride came to be called "Russian Mountains."

The French made the season of coaster-riding longer by establishing the first wheeled coaster in Paris in 1804. The name "Russian Mountains" was used. In 1817 the famous Aerial Walk opened at nearby Beaujon Garden. Its many improvements and safety devices soon made the old 1804 ride outdated.

The first roller coaster in the United States was an inclined railway used to carry coal down to Mauch Chunk, Pennsylvania. In 1870 it was converted to haul passengers to the top of Mt. Pisgah, then drop them at a rate of 60 feet (18 meters) to the mile. Certainly a slow pace, but the ride through the mountains was a grand experience.

It took the engineering skills of LaMarcus A. Thompson to make a device like the Mauch

One of the rides typical of earlier roller coasters

Chunk Railway work at an amusement park. He became known as the "father of gravity"—and invented one type of roller coaster used in amusement parks. Thompson put in a simple machine called "the Switchback Railway" at Brooklyn's Coney Island in 1884. Cars ran down a wavy track and rarely went faster than 6 miles (10 kilometers) per hour. Attendants then pushed the cars up the next hill for a return ride. It was crude but

very popular. A day's income totaled $700 (at 5 cents a ride), and Thompson had more orders than he could fill.

Also, at Coney Island, Captain Paul Boyton installed an odd machine called the "Beecher" or "Flip-Flap Coaster." On this rickety nightmare, cars performed a 360-degree somersault. Only the blessings of centrifugal force clamped the cars to the tracks—and the passengers to their seats. People often complained of uncomfortable neck strain and stopped using this coaster. Soon the ride was taken down.

In 1901 Edward Prescott's Loop-the-Loop became the talk of Coney Island. Instead of the Flip-Flap's true circle, the new ride successfully used an oval track and removed those uncomfortable strains. The success was short-lived. Many did not believe that the ride was better, even though a glass of water on test runs failed to spill a drop.

The public changed its mind completely in 1927 when a horrendous roller coaster called the "Cyclone" opened at Crystal Beach in Ontario, Canada. Some 75,000 people knocked down railings to get a good look the first day of its run.

Designed by Harry Guy

Traver, it was billed as "The Most Fearsome Coaster Ever Built." The vice president of Crystal Beach recalls that "the Cyclone was a wicked ride. Before the last cars left the top of the first hill, the front car had already started on a bank. Every turn twisted sharply, and there was a figure eight that the cars ran at top speed. The Cyclone is the only coaster that I have heard of that had a nurse manning a first-aid station."

People came from all over the world to watch. Some dared to ride. Those who did often fainted, and broken ribs from flying elbows were not unusual.

PATH OF THE CYCLONE

Palisades Park, on the Hudson River across from Manhattan, had watched the Canadian Cyclone's opening with great interest. Palisades needed something to outdo the popular coasters at Brooklyn's Coney Island. So, in 1928, Palisades Park opened a monster identical to the first one at Crystal Beach. In an editorial about it for the *New York Telegram,* Robert Garland wrote: "As a connoisseur of roller coasters, I advise you to consult a doctor before you climb aboard the new Cyclone at Palisades Park. . . . That Cyclone doesn't play fair. It drags you up an incline, tosses you down the other side, turns you over this way, turns you over that way, and . . . shoots you to the stars again."

Working with Frank Church, Harry Traver also put together a masterpiece at Playland Park, Rye Beach, New York. Aptly named the "Aero-Coaster," it was the greatest body-wringer and the most violent ride ever built. It was not only 90 feet (27 meters) high, but its first drop was 10 feet (3 meters) below ground. It looped continually and never stopped grinding until it reached the platform.

The late Roaring Twenties saw the coaster business boom. Aviation pioneers, including the Wright Brothers, admired these coasters' speed, curves and drops. Charles Lindbergh (who once worked in an amusement park) reportedly said that "the Cyclone was a greater thrill than flying an airplane at top speed!"

Suddenly, the Depression hit. The next 30 years saw 1300 roller coasters ground under by bulldozers or left to rot. Even Harry Traver's Cyclones were leveled—not an easy job, since the wrecker's ball, weather,

Coney Island advertised a variety of amusements accommodating thrill-seekers.

bulldozers and dynamite barely budged them. Crystal Beach finally decided to use some of the structuring and wooden parts in a new, mostly steel, coaster. The wood and steel remains have become a shrine for roller-coaster buffs.

IN THE CYCLONE'S WAKE

How do the rides of today compare with those famous coasters? Many will say the rides built in the 1960s and 1970s make the older coasters look like child's play. Others will tell you that no amount of money spent could create a new machine to equal the thrills, cleverness and craftsmanship of the older rides. One yardstick exists. The 1927 Cyclone still stands on Surf Avenue at Coney Island. By any measure—including today's wax-smooth rides—it is a masterpiece. This machine is 80-foot (24-meter) proof that the coasters of the Twenties were the finest ever made.

Outstanding among today's coaster designers is John Allen, formerly of the Philadelphia Toboggan Company. His masterpiece is probably the Mister Twister at Elitch's Gardens in Denver, Colorado. Almost 100 feet (30 meters) high, it is crammed with hills and curves and has the best tunnel ride anywhere. Many list it as the finest roller coaster standing today.

The Associated Press lists the Texas Cyclone at Astroworld in Houston, Texas, as the last word in roller coasters. A close second is the Thunderbolt at Kennywood Park near Pittsburgh. It uses a natural valley to hide the most frightening parts of the ride. The final drops of 80 feet (24 meters) and 90 feet (27 meters) make its finish the most shattering in the world.

Yet it's not the finish, or the first drop, or the curves that sets a great roller coaster apart from the others. It's the pacing—the way the speed, hills, curves, tunnels and finish are combined. "We build in psychology," says designer John Allen. "Part of the appeal is the imagined danger. That's why riders start screaming before the car even takes off."

The ride up the first hill is slow on purpose. The car is allowed to dangle at the top so that you can study the view—for miles—and savor the supposed terrors ahead. Then down it goes. The thrill comes, not from the speed, but from speeding up in seconds from 5 to 60 miles (8 to 97 kilometers) per hour, into a state of weightlessness. That's the glory—or horror.

Riders experiencing the "glory or—horror" of coaster speed

Every effort is made to make a roller coaster seem terrifying; yet the ride is among the safest at an amusement park. The fear that cars will jump the track and that the passengers will be thrown out is unfounded. The cars cannot jump the track because undertrack wheels prevent their flying upward, and side friction wheels keep them on course. An iron bar locked across the passenger's lap can be released only by an attendant or by a special device. None of these safety factors impress the rider. The illusion is one of danger and excitement.

Despite all care taken to ensure riders' safety, major accidents do happen. Passengers change seats in mid-ride. They stand; they perform balancing acts on sharp curves. "We just have to figure the customer as an accident looking for a place to happen," says a former Coney Island operator. Fortunately, not all mishaps are serious.

At Conneaut Lake in western Pennsylvania, the coaster entered a dark tunnel midway through the ride. Nightmarish screams could be heard for miles as the cars echoed through the dark depths. The screams continued until the train reached the unloading platform. Passengers flew off the cars, stumbling, arms flying, gasping for breath. Onlookers stared in alarm. Coaster attendants rushed to the aid of the distressed riders. The front car had hit a skunk.

Most mishaps involve belongings: wallets, wigs, hats and keys are often lost. Operators say they find enough loose change under the tracks to keep them going into the winter months. False teeth were found under the Cyclone at Coney Island.

Has the best possible roller coaster been built? No. Is there a limit to what the designers have planned for our minds and bodies? No again. Walt Disney World opened its 175-foot (53-meter)-high Space Mountain in 1975 at a cost that was more than that of Disneyland in 1955. James Irwin, lunar module pilot of Apollo 15, calls it rougher than Saturn V.

Knotts Berry Farm in California has premiered its Corkscrew Coaster. Based on the 1901 Loop-the-Loop, it drops passengers at 75 feet (23 meters) into two 360-degree somersaults. Nearby, at Magic Mountain, the Great American Revolution coaster features a ghastly up-and-down loop 70 feet (21 meters) high.

In the Ultimate Roller Coaster competition, three Fairchild test engineers submitted the KG-135 research plane. It won hands down. Height: start at 25,000 feet (7620 meters), peak at 35,000 feet (10,688 meters); distance—9 miles (15 kilometers) horizontally in 70 seconds for each completed curve. These figures were shown to a coaster designer. He roared, then headed for the drawing board.

Number of Words: 1821 ÷ _____ Minutes Reading Time = Rate _____

Bigger and "better" roller coasters
are always being imagined and built.

I. SKIMMING

Match each roller coaster with its location. Skim the story for the information. Write the letter of your answer from column B in the space provided in column A.

	A		B
_____ 1.	the first Cyclone	**a.**	Astroworld in Houston
_____ 2.	the Rebel Yell	**b.**	Knotts Berry Farms in California
_____ 3.	the Aerial Walk	**c.**	Crystal Beach in Ontario, Canada
_____ 4.	Mister Twister	**d.**	Beaujon Garden in France
_____ 5.	the Texas Cyclone	**e.**	Walt Disney World in Florida
_____ 6.	Space Mountain	**f.**	Elitch's Gardens in Denver
_____ 7.	the Corkscrew Coaster	**g.**	Kings Dominion near Richmond, Virginia

5 points for each correct answer   SCORE: _____

II. INFERENCES

Some information in the story is not stated directly. Check √ four conclusions that can be reasonably drawn from the story.

_____ **1.**   The people who ride roller coasters are mostly teenagers.

_____ **2.**   It is not easy to decide which roller coaster offers the best possible ride.

_____ **3.**   A roller coaster ride is not as dangerous as it seems.

_____ **4.** Designers keep producing better and more thrilling roller coasters.

_____ **5.** Few people would go to an amusement park if it did not have a roller coaster.

_____ **6.** Roller coasters will continue to be popular.

10 points for each correct answer   SCORE: _____

III. FACT/OPINION

Decide whether each statement below is fact (F) or an opinion (O).

_____ **1.** The best roller coaster in the world is the Texas Cyclone.

_____ **2.** You should consult a doctor before climbing on a roller coaster.

_____ **3.** Originally, roller coasters were just ice slides and "Russian Mountains."

_____ **4.** People who ride roller coasters enjoy feeling scared.

_____ **5.** The 1927 Cyclone still stands on Surf Avenue at Coney Island.

5 points for each correct answer   SCORE: _____

IV. QUESTIONS FOR THOUGHT

What makes a good roller coaster ride? How would you design the best roller coaster in the world? Explain your choices.

Doctor for the People

Elizabeth Levy and Mara Miller

She is a broad-boned and wide-shouldered smiling figure in a white doctor's coat. That coat must be famous among Nashville cleaners because, throughout our interview, Dr. Dorothy Brown jots down names, numbers and notes to herself on the hem of her coat.

Dr. Brown is 59 years old, black and a woman—the first black woman to practice general surgery in the South. She is also the first black woman to win an election and sit in the Tennessee State Legislature.

Her story, however, is not on the hem of her lab coat. "When I was a youngster, I was a complete extrovert, growing up in a sea of white people. I was in an orphanage in Troy, New York, with about 350 kids, and only six of us were blacks. If you had enough colds during the school year, when school closed you were selected to have your tonsils and adenoids out. When I was five, they sent me to the hospital for that. I caused quite a stir. I insisted that I wanted to make the rounds with the nurses, and I wanted to use the doctor's stethoscope and carry my chart into the operating room.

"You see, I was completely oblivious to the business of race. I was enthusiastic and enthralled by the sights and smells of medicine. I wanted to be a doctor from then on. I didn't even think in terms of being a nurse. I wanted to be the chief head-knocker.

"Nobody laughed at me. At that orphanage we were encouraged constantly to assess what we wanted to become. So when I was five and said I wanted to become a doctor, there was no one to say, 'Why, that's insane! Why don't you be more practical?' "

"There was a policy at the orphanage that when black kids reached about 14 or 15, they'd be farmed out to work in the wealthy homes in the neighborhood to learn how to be cooks, maids and butlers.

"During the summers and after school, I was working as a maid. All the people I worked for knew I was trying to save money for college. So when I said to them, 'Will you let me try to do a whole day's work in just a half a day, but pay me for the whole day?' they agreed. The work was very heavy physically and quite demanding.

"One day this lady I worked for told me that the Methodist Women of the Troy Conference was looking for a black girl to send to Bennett College in Greensboro, North Carolina, all expenses paid. The all-black college was named for a local Troy minister, and in all the years, the Methodist Women had never sponsored a black student—well, we were 'Negroes' at that time—they had never had a Negro girl attend this college. So I met with them in the middle of August, and when they took me down on the train on the second day of September, they said, 'We don't know you very well, Dorothy, but we hope you're the right girl.' So that's how I got to college."

After college, Ms. Brown

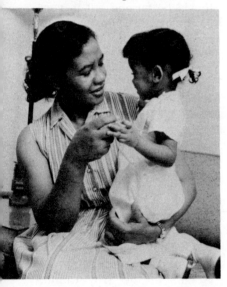

Dr. Brown and her daughter

trained at the Meharry Medical College in Nashville. Then she came back north to intern at Harlem Hospital in New York.

"At the end of my internship I sought a residency in general surgery at Harlem Hospital. Of course, that was insane. They were just not going to have a woman. So I turned to Meharry, where I had done my medical training. Matthew Walker, who was chief of surgery, was a little amused, but he asked his staff anyway. Of course they said that a woman could not withstand the physical rigors of five years of training in general surgery.

"But I was pretty insistent, and so Dr. Walker decided to try me. There were no rigors whatsoever. Of course, there were not going to be any as far as I was concerned, because I was bound, bent and determined that, if necessary, I would overcompensate to see to it that I made it.

"I'll never forget one Saturday night when I was chief resident in general surgery and I had just finished a series of emergency cases with an assistant. We were on our way over to the cafeteria and then were going to go get some sleep.

"All of a sudden, the Emergency Room had another case, and this fellow who was going to assist me turned and said, 'Dee, I hate to admit this to you, but I just can't go any further.'

"I was tired too, but I said, 'That's okay, just go on ahead.' It was just fortunate that I was the mule who could carry on. There was no crying or getting emotionally disturbed, because I knew the job I had to do, and I went forward to do it.

"Since that episode, my word to women students is that when you pass through the doors at seven or eight in the morning, you are not a woman, you're a doctor.

"I had one man, an elderly man who had a preoperative diagnosis of a ruptured appendix. I was chief resident at the time, which means that I had nine to eleven fellows working under me. But, of course, as chief resident and being more experienced, I was charged with doing the surgery on the poor-risk cases. So I went around to the ward to take a look at this poor-risk old gent before I operated on him, and he looked up at me and said, 'You're not going to operate on me?'

"I said, 'Oh, yes, I am, sir.'

"He said, 'You'd better get one of these fellows to operate on me because you ain't nothing but a little old girl, and you don't know what you're doing.'

"I said, 'Okay.' I let the fellows go on and work him up, and I just waited until he got to the operating room, then I operated on him. . . . I told him afterward.

Dr. Brown entertaining some young friends

"I recall when I began private practice, one of the doctors said, 'Dee, I wouldn't start to practice medicine in Nashville. People are not accustomed to a woman surgeon; you'll starve to death.' But it hasn't happened. My first year of practice,

I had about 40 percent male and 60 percent female patients. Right now I have as many male patients as I have females. And though most of them are black, I have a fair share of whites, too, even though my office is in the black community.

"Of course, I've had to beat the bushes looking for my own surgical cases. If I sat back and waited for referrals, I probably *would* starve. So I do a lot of general medicine practice too. I just see anybody who wants to see a doctor. If it's something I can handle, then I go ahead and do it; if it's something I don't want to handle, then I refer them. What I want to do is to perform surgery.

"One of the reasons I went into a specialty instead of going into the immensity of general practice was that I was just too afraid I didn't know enough medicine to save enough people.

"There's no use my telling a lie. When I lose a patient, I spend the rest of that night going through that patient's records to see if I have made a mistake, to see if there wasn't something else that I could have done that would have spelled the difference between life and death. These things weigh upon me, and I think this is one of the reasons that I work so hard."

Because she was so well known in the community, Dr. Brown was asked to run for the seat in Nashville's predominantly black state lower-house district. Although some of the local political bosses were against her, she won both the primary and the general election with ease, and became the first black woman in the Tennessee Legislature.

"I feel there are certain things, certain issues, that you have to address yourself to in this life, and if you're rational about it, then don't turn back.

"No, I haven't accepted defeat, not in my entire life," says Dr. Brown. "The only defeat I understand is physical defeat. To me it's a grievous sin for people to waste the days of their lives, and not to do something that makes the world a little better, or at least notifies the world that you've been around."

Dr. Brown exemplifies this credo.

Number of Words: 1435 ÷ _____ Minutes Reading Time = Rate _____

I. SEQUENCE

Five events in Dorothy Brown's life are listed below. Number them in the order in which they happened in her life.

_____ **a.** She attended Meharry Medical College.

_____ **b.** She won a seat in the State Legislature.

_____ **c.** She became chief of surgery at Riverside Hospital.

_____ **d.** She attended Bennett College.

_____ **e.** She became an intern at Harlem Hospital.

7 points for each correct answer   SCORE: _____

II. CHARACTERIZATION

Check ✓ three statements below that describe the life or character of Dorothy Brown.

_____ **1.** Throughout her life, she has been very strong-willed, and has reached many goals she set for herself.

_____ **2.** She was discouraged by difficulties.

_____ **3.** She would not have been able to achieve what she did if she had lived in another part of the country.

_____ **4.** It was more difficult for her to become a surgeon than simply a doctor.

_____ **5.** In Nashville, people came to accept her as a good doctor.

10 points for each correct answer   SCORE: _____

III. VOCABULARY

Write the letter of the word or phrase that means the same as the word in italics.

_____ 1. Since she was such an *extrovert*, she made it a point to talk to everyone.
   a. an easy-going person   **b.** an outgoing person
   c. a stranger

_____ 2. We walked on, *oblivious* to the strong, rising wind.
   a. fully aware of   **b.** not paying attention to
   c. worrying about

_____ 3. The pop singer kept us *enthralled* for hours; but the folk singer put us to sleep.
   a. spellbound   **b.** waiting   **c.** yawning

5 points for each correct answer   SCORE: _____

IV. LANGUAGE USAGE

Dr. Brown shows a lot about herself through what she says. Match each quotation (a, b, c or d) with its actual meaning below.

a. My mind was made up.   **c.** I searched hard.
b. I was ambitious.   **d.** I was strong.

_____ 1. I wanted to be the chief head-knocker.
_____ 2. I was bound, bent, and determined.
_____ 3. I was the mule who could carry on.
_____ 4. I had to beat the bushes.

5 points for each correct answer   SCORE: _____

PERFECT TOTAL SCORE: 100   TOTAL SCORE: _____

V. QUESTION FOR THOUGHT

What difficulties can you imagine in realizing your goal?

A HOME

You may raise your own children in a home that will be a hollow, glass-and-aluminum cylinder over 400 feet (122 meters) in diameter, bent into a circle 3.5 miles (5.6 kilometers) around and over 1 mile (1.6 kilometers) across. The structure will look like a huge bicycle wheel.

Television producers are not the only ones who think that men and women will be living in space by 1999. Scientists have already made detailed plans for building a city in space where 10,000 people could live, play and work. The orbiting space colony will produce energy from solar-

IN SPACE

The Editors of *Boys' Life*

powered electric generating stations. It will beam this energy to earth for sale.

In order to copy earth's gravity, the wheel will turn about its hub once each minute. The outward forces that make it turn will give a feeling of weight. Everyone will walk with feet outward and head toward the center of the wheel. But they won't feel strange.

The wheel shape was chosen for comfort, safety and efficiency where a greater mix of neighborhoods, views and scenes could be built.

Mix and change will be important in space to keep you from becoming bored. The inside of the space colony will use Japanese gardening styles: hidden nooks and corners, surprising and sudden changes of scenery, and clever use of plants and buildings on a small scale. Life will be like that of apartment dwellers in modern condominiums.

To protect against cosmic rays, solar wind, solar flares and other dangerous radiations found in space, a thick shield of dirt and cinder block will be needed. The materials for this will be mined on the moon. Since the shield will be heavy, the part of the station where people live will rotate inside the shield.

There is almost eight times more sunlight in space than on earth. It will provide electricity, lighting and heat and will also be used for farming.

Farming in space may turn out to be easier than on earth. By controlling the amounts of sunlight, carbon dioxide, water, temperature and the length of the growing season, plants can be made to grow much faster. Our space farmers should be able to grow enough for all 10,000 people and their livestock (cattle, sheep, goats, fish) on less than 160 acres (65 hectares), the size of a single small American family farm.

Although your weight will be normal in the place where you live, you won't have weight in the center of the wheel. This hub will be mainly for play. It will also be used for space ships to dock.

The space colony will cost a lot of money to build and operate. Can it pay its own way? Important to its economic success is the fact that the people who live there will be able to make glass, aluminum, titanium, iron, silicon and oxygen. The raw materials will come mostly from the moon. The settlers can use dirt scooped off the surface. They will not need to do much deep mining or looking for minerals.

A space colony is no longer a dream. Scientists say its perfection is now possible and only a matter of time. It is a fact that people no longer need to be tied to this planet.

Number of Words: 548 ÷ _____ Minutes Reading Time = Rate _____

I. OUTLINING

Complete the following outline of the selection. Write each sentence from the list in its proper place below.

1. Crops can grow there.
2. The city will produce its own energy.
3. People will live there.

I. Scientists have planned a city in space.
    A. The city will orbit high in space.
    B. _____
    C. _____
II. The orbiting city will be self-sufficient.
    A. Livestock will be raised.
    B. _____

10 points for each correct answer   SCORE: _____

II. CLASSIFYING

Indicate whether each of the items below is necessary for survival (A) or comfort (B) in the space city. Put a check ✓ in the correct column.

	A	B
1. gardens	_____	_____
2. neighborhoods	_____	_____
3. solar energy	_____	_____
4. farming areas	_____	_____
5. wheel-shaped	_____	_____
6. gravity	_____	_____
7. dirt and cinder wall	_____	_____
8. small-scale environment	_____	_____

5 points for each correct answer   SCORE: _____

III. FACT/OPINION

Write (F) if the statement is based on fact. Write (O) if the statement is based on opinion.

_____ 1. With controlled conditions plants can be made to grow faster.

_____ 2. Japanese gardeners are quite clever.

_____ 3. Space farmers should be able to grow enough food to feed the colonists.

_____ 4. Space colonists will be living in space by the year 1999.

_____ 5. A thick shield of dirt and cinders will be built to protect the space colonists.

6 points for each correct answer   SCORE: _____

PERFECT TOTAL SCORE: 100   TOTAL SCORE: _____

IV. QUESTIONS FOR THOUGHT

Describe what things you would like to take with you from Earth to a space colony. Why? What would you like to leave behind? Why?

He Dives After Treasure

Stephen C. Michaud

Along an eastern Mediterranean sea-lane, used regularly by merchants and navies for at least 5000 years, is the resort town of Bodrum, Turkey. A jumble of hotels and discos fronts a busy harbor shared by one of the largest sponge-fishing fleets in the Mediterranean.

Sponge fishing can be dreary and dangerous work. But the ugly-looking sponges are not all that the Bodrum fishermen have brought up with their nets. For centuries, they have returned to port with bits and pieces of glass, pottery or sculpture fused together. Scores and scores of *amphorae,* or very old two-handled clay jugs, are often found whole. These jugs are seen all over, and fishermen use them at home to hold wine or water. It has been this way since before recorded history.

No one went looking for those jugs on purpose. Their very size long ago made historians and archeologists believe that the waters off Bodrum hid a large number of wrecked ships from the past 5000 years. These ships were probably swamped or dashed on the rocks by the sudden, evil summer winds.

All these finds and all the scuba divers' reports showed that tons of cargo, or freight, were spread across the sea floor. But archeologists had not been able to tap them in this setting under the sea.

Enter Peter Throckmorton, American writer, photographer and expert diver who, in the late 1950s, set out to look into this huge undersea graveyard. With the aid of a friend, a local sponge fisherman, Throckmorton found out where dozens of wrecks were

A scuba diver surfacing off a Mediterrean resort town with treasure from an ancient shipwreck

along the Turkish coast. From the pieces of art he brought back, Throckmorton reasoned that at least some of the pieces dated from the Late Bronze Age (3500 B.C.).

One wreck in particular caught Throckmorton's interest. It lay in 100 feet (30 meters) of water off Cape Gelidonya, a deserted headland 150 miles (241 kilometers) down the coast from Bodrum. Tools and copper bars that he brought back from the site—plus a few pieces of broken pottery—were strong proof that this was a craft from the time of Homer's heroes, the oldest shipwreck ever found.

It was a 3200-year-old time capsule, waiting to reveal its secrets. But Turkish divers for sunken cargo, who knew the wreck contained copper and bronze, were making ready to dynamite it into usable bits.

In only six months, the Cape Gelidonya wreck would be lost to history. Throckmorton went to New York in December 1959 for an important meeting of the Archeological Institute of America. There he met George F. Bass.

At a meeting with Bass and others, Throckmorton made his case for digging up the ship. He backed his claims with photographs of artifacts (simple objects that are very old) that the archaeologists found hard to pass up. The man who had dug up the ancient city of Gordion in Anatolian Turkey made up his mind: the wreck would be excavated, and George Bass would do it. First, however, Bass must learn to dive.

"I jumped at the offer," Bass now recalls. "I was too innocent to know what the problems might be."

In 1960 Throckmorton set about putting together a diving team, while the University of Pennsylvania Museum's director, Froelich Rainey, went looking for money to support the project. Bass took a YMCA scuba course, managing to cram ten weeks of practice into six, and then popped down to his native South Carolina to marry the music student he had met the summer before. They left for Turkey two days later.

The camp hugged the base of a cliff where light-gray stone collected and aimed the sun's rays down on the tents. But this place had the only source of drinking water. The team of eight dived from a rented boat. Only when the group had finished its first dives did Bass see how big his task would be.

Whatever it was, 100 feet (30 meters) down, the ship was larger than they had guessed. Great hunks of copper and bronze lay melted together at the bottom. The sand moved from place to place, time and again hiding the site. The team could only guess the ship's outline from neat little piles of tools or pots.

As an archeologist, Bass was schooled in patience and the value of the scientific approach. So since there were no footsteps to follow, nautical archeology got started in much the same way as it had started on dry land. But instead of brushing sand away from their finds, these scientists sucked relics to the surface with a compressed-air pipe built quickly at the site. Sand and debris came up through the pipe, and a homemade basket caught larger objects.

Group members mapped and drew the wreck on plastic tablets carried below. A diver with a camera swam slowly over the wreck doing "aerial mapping" and marking his position with a plumb line. A balloon was used to lift heavy objects from the deep waters.

Bass and his team dug up the site completely and brought back with them detailed drawings and photographs of the ancient wreck. (The artifacts stayed in Turkey at the Bodrum Museum of Marine Antiquities, established by Throckmorton.) Then followed seven years of research through archives and records. Bass was able to establish that the ship was built by the Canaanites. It was used to trade copper and bronze which the captain melted and made into bars as the ship sailed. Bass even learned the ports of call.

Archeologist Bass and aide with artifact retrieved from deep sea wreck

The Bass team had shown that the study of underwater archeology was possible and that it could be done without professional divers. Most important, when Bass studied the Gelidonya wreck, he found out that there is much information lying at the bottom of the sea.

"For one thing," he says, "it became clear that most of our classical bronzes were going to come from the sea. The ships themselves would be good to study. Think of what they carried! Anything that anyone ever made, I think, has been carried at one time or another on a ship. These things are very well kept and very well dated. The most important reason is that they have been kept away from people. In the past humans have liked to melt down metal statues, burn marble statues for lime, melt down gold coins for earrings, chop up ships for firewood."

As a result of his find, Bass received more funds from the

Bass team aboard fishing boat off Turkish coast

Museum and a team of young archeologists who were trained to dive. They returned to Turkey to continue their work. The new site, which Throckmorton had also discovered earlier, lay 130 feet (40 meters) down on a slope, under a rock ledge that had torn out the bottoms of at least a dozen ships over the centuries. The nearest land was a miserable rock called Yassi Ada (Turkish for "flat island") that had no fresh water. The only living

Archeological diver makes his or her way to underwater telephone booth and decompression chamber.

things were thistles and a growing number of hungry rats. Yassi Ada became the campsite for the group.

Now Bass had two local fishing boats to work from and a diving barge. Throughout the 1960s, digging through the Byzantine wreck and a nearby Roman site grew less and less simple. Not only were the archeologists now familiar with the dangers and problems of their special work, but the team developed a wide variety of scientific aids.

Mapping was improved by adding a metal grid over the wreck, which let the team divide the site into four coded parts. Bass helped perfect a way to make underwater graphs of the wreck. An underwater telephone booth was put in along with a decompression chamber. This room let divers spend a longer time on the site. Side-scanning sonar was used for the first time to find old hulks and artifacts hidden by the sand. Bass even used a specially designed two-man submarine, the *Asherah*, fitted with a television camera and photo-mapping equipment in her work.

The 70-odd gold and copper coins found in the wreck gave Bass a good idea of when the ship sank. The coin dates stopped suddenly at A.D. 625, probably the year the ship went down. From that bench mark, the mass of pottery on board was easily dated.

With his larger team and the aid of experts in everything from ship modeling to post-classical Greek civilization, Bass set up the last voyage of an ancient vessel, this time with exacting detail. "It is now the most information ever gotten out of an ancient wreck," he says. "We know how much money they had and what its spending power was. We know where the ship was coming from, how much it cost and how it was constructed."

Nautical archeology expanded beyond Turkey in 1967. A member of Bass's team, graduate student Michael L. Katzev, and his wife, Susan, left for Cyprus, where they conducted the excavation of the only classical Greek ship—a late 4th century B.C. merchant vessel—ever found. They not only excavated the site off the town of Kyrenia, but also brought the nearly intact hull to the surface. A special museum in Kyrenia now exhibits it.

Elsewhere, other archeologists followed Bass's lead and sought out his help with their digs. Yet, as nautical archeology arrived, its founder began having grave misgivings. One of Bass's closest colleagues and friends had been stricken with a blood clot and nearly lost his life at Yassi Ada in 1969. Bass had also seen a Turkish sponge diver die in the expedition's decompression chamber (a place where the body can get adjusted to changes in pressure) while undergoing treatment for decompression sickness, or the bends.

Bass took four years off to do some further studies and, with the aid and encouragement of his wife, Ann, who takes nautical archeology as seriously as he does, Bass founded the American Institute of Nautical Archeology (now the Institute of Nautical Archaeology). Of the two dozen or so archeologists in the world who are well trained enough to undertake an underwater dig, fully half are INA staff members.

The digs continue, and some surprising finds have been made off the coasts of Italy and Kenya. In 1976, at Yorktown, Virginia, the INA team dove on what they believe to have been one of Lord Cornwallis' ships that most likely sank in the last battle of the Revolutionary War. The studies are still going on at the mouth of the Penobscot River in Maine. There, in 1779, the largest fleet of warships assembled by the American side during the Revolution was turned away by just a few British ships.

The new home of INA is at Texas A & M University. Says Bass, "I'm staying in nautical archeology because I think it's going to turn up some tremendously exciting historical results. I'm really past the point where I get excited about diving itself. I'm really bored with jumping in a wet suit and diving into cold water. I don't enjoy the headaches. But I guess my dream as a prehistorian is to find a Stone Age ship, an Early Bronze Age ship, a ship from ancient Crete. I know they will be found, maybe not in my lifetime, but they're certainly there."

Number of Words: 1889 ÷ _____ Minutes Reading Time = Rate _____

Some surprising finds are being made off the coasts of Italy and Kenya.

I. AUTHOR'S PURPOSE

Check ✓ three phrases which explain why the author wrote the story.

_____ **1.** to describe Bass' experiences as a nautical archeologist

_____ **2.** to criticize the field of nautical archeology

_____ **3.** to explain why archeology is a rich person's pastime

_____ **4.** to show how nautical archeology has grown in 25 years

_____ **5.** to describe George Bass' career in nautical archeology

10 points for each correct answer   SCORE: _____

II. CLASSIFYING

The selection mentions many types of ships. Complete each of the following sentences below using the letter of one of the following ships named.

a. warship(s)   **c.** diving barge(s)
b. cargo vessel(s)   **d.** submarine(s)

1. Ships that carry goods are called _____.

2. When the expeditions got bigger, a _____ was brought to the sites.

3. To map and photograph wrecks from up close, a _____ was used.

4. In 1779, a fleet of American _____ was sunk off Maine.

10 points for each correct answer   SCORE: _____

III. CAUSE/EFFECT

Nautical archeology has been very successful. Match each cause (column A) for this success to its effect (column B).

	A		**B**
_____ 1.	Thousands of old ships lie under the sea.	**a.**	The sites can be reached fairly easily.
_____ 2.	Many ships sank near land, and in shallow water.	**b.**	The details on many objects have not been erased or destroyed.
_____ 3.	Sonar scans can locate large things more easily than a shovel.	**c.**	The number of objects that could be recovered is enormous.
_____ 4.	Most shipwrecks remain lost.	**d.**	Everything that a ship carried is still available for study.
_____ 5.	Stone and metal objects have been well preserved.	**e.**	Wrecks that might remain hidden by sand can be located and explored.

6 points for each correct answer   SCORE: _____

PERFECT TOTAL SCORE: 100   TOTAL SCORE: _____

IV. QUESTIONS FOR THOUGHT

What would you hope to find in diving for old, wrecked ships? What would you do with your discoveries?

Tung Is My Name

Tseng Pei-yao

The painting, completed in 1973, brought jeers from the villagers—and attracted the attention of art critics.

"Suddenly he said he wasn't going to work anymore. He would spend the rest of his life painting," said his wife. "And he wanted me to support the family."

It was a few days after Hung Tung's 50th birthday. In his hut in Nan Kun Shen, a tiny Chinese village about an hour's drive from Tainan City, on the Nationalist Chinese island of Taiwan, this farmer, who could

not read or write, was watching his youngest son practice calligraphy, the art of lettering. To Hung, the characters looked like human or animal shapes. Without thinking, he picked up a felt-tip pen and started to draw, adding heads and limbs so that the shapes looked even more human. He was so happy and excited that he skipped supper. When he had finished working, an entire exercise book was full of similar sketches. Neither Hung nor his wife had any idea that this was the beginning of a career that would make him famous all over the country.

A few years later, in March 1976, Hung Tung's work was shown at Lincoln Centre in Taipei. Lines formed around the building. A reporter remarked, "He packs in a greater crowd than the moon rocks the astronauts brought back." This was certainly a change for Hung whose life had been very simple and quiet up to then.

Hung Tung's parents had died when he was a child. He had been raised by an uncle who was too poor to send him to school. Hung worked in neighbors' fields and fish ponds when he was a teenager. At 25 he married Liu Lai-jou, and the couple made a living growing melons, maize and peanuts. Three sons and two daughters came swiftly. Hung Tung worked in neighbors' fields to earn extra income, while his wife sold souvenirs at the village temple.

But after 25 years, he refused to do such work any more. In a tiny room in his hut, Hung would paint through the night. By and by, he made a studio from a deserted pigsty. When he begged his wife to buy him paper, brushes and paint, the poor woman borrowed money from neighbors.

When Hung Tung displayed his paintings outside the village temple, the villagers asked, "Is this man crazy? Our children can scribble better than that!"

Hung Tung covered the walls and door of his home with colorful dragons, flowers and delicately drawn Chinese symbols that no one could read. On an arch in front of his hut, he built a wooden cross. People started to say that he had been touched by the supernatural.

"I paint what's in my heart, and I feel good," he said. "Why should anyone understand?"

Perhaps the only one in the family who understood Hung Tung was his eldest son, Hung Yen, a factory worker. Yen gave gifts of painting materials to his father. The years had been tough for this man. Yen felt that it was time for his father to enjoy life.

But then Yen died of a liver disease, and Hung Tung became quiet. He didn't like to be with people very much. It was a very sad-faced man who called at my home in Tainan one hot July day in 1970. "I wonder if I could ask what you think of some paintings?" he said. As an art teacher, I was struck by the energy of the odd forms, vivid colors and complex line drawings. I told Hung Tung that I found the work very different from anyone else's, and it had a special strength. I said that he should urge the painter to keep working hard.

"There is hope for me?" the man asked, his face lighting up. Shyly, he confessed that he had painted the pictures.

For almost two years, Hung Tung came to my studio every Sunday. I introduced him to new painting materials and methods and gave advice about his work. Tung was filled with curiosity and caught on quickly. Perhaps what he looked for most was the self-confidence he had lost through the jeers of the villagers.

First he painted on the red scroll paper used for Chinese celebrations. Later, he worked on cotton paper and canvas. He painted women with red, green

One of Hung Tung's early paintings, this collection of colorful faces is painted on red scroll paper.

and yellow faces; fish and leaves growing out of heads; palace-like buildings; geometric forms and plants.

Although none of his paintings have names, some have simple words like "sun," "moon," "hill" written on them. It is impossible to make out the meaning of many words. "I invent words that belong to me," Tung said. Perhaps, he was working hard at trying to read and write the language.

In 1972 a reporter from Echo magazine saw Hung Tung's colorful paintings with their odd, new forms. He wrote an article about "the mad artist" that attracted the attention of the art world in Taipei. Other magazines and newspapers began to publish reports about the the old man and his great works of art. Some said that Hung Tung was like the American artist Grandma Moses.

Since he began to paint in 1970, Hung Tung has refused to sell the hundreds of paintings he has produced because "they are like my flesh and blood," he

explains. But not long ago, he decided to sell a large number because he was sick and needed the money.

Hung Tung's paintings continue to win respect. Says art critic Ho Cheng Kwang, editor of Artist Magazine: "Hung Tung's works show the mind of an "old" child—pure and innocent. But he also has a patience, color sense, and way of painting that are not found in children's art."

Are his paintings the work of a genius or a madman? Another famous Chinese artist, Liu Chi-wei, says: "Hung Tung pours out a frightening kind of creativity. He puts down the real world and praises his own. It is true art."

It was a glorious day for Hung Tung when he met the press in Taipei the day before his exhibit opened. He arrived almost an hour late, wearing a shirt he had painted himself. The back of this shirt had a picture of an old man beating a drum with a stone. "The sound is 'Tung' and that's my name," he announced.

Number of Words: 1054 ÷ _____ Minutes Reading Time = Rate _____

I. SUPPORTING DETAILS

Check ✓ the two story details that describe Tung's painting.

_____ **1.**   He was a poor farmer who could not read or write.

_____ **2.**   He had never been to art school, but he learned to use new materials and techniques quickly.

_____ **3.**   His work shows the mind of an "old child": innocent, but with a special strength that is not like a child's.

_____ **4.**   He paints what is in his heart, not the outside world.

_____ **5.**   He has always wanted to be famous as a painter.

---

5 points for each correct answer   SCORE: _____

II. AUTHOR'S PURPOSE

Check ✓ the phrase (a, b or c) that correctly completes each statement below.

1.   In describing Tung's work, the author wants to show that Tung
_____ **a.** is not a very unusual painter.
_____ **b.** has developed his own style of painting.
_____ **c.** will only be famous during his own lifetime.

2.   The author mentions that Tung had to beg for paints and paper in order to show that the artist
_____ **a.** expected other people to do things for him.
_____ **b.** was not a proud man.
_____ **c.** desperately wanted to go on painting.

3.   The author describes the villagers' reaction to Tung's paintings to show that people
_____ **a.** did not understand his work.
_____ **b.** did not like him.
_____ **c.** thought he was a genius.

4. The author describes his reaction to the paintings to show
   _____ **a.** that Tung is a clever art teacher.
   _____ **b.** how unimpressing they are.
   _____ **c.** he thinks Tung is a talented artist.

10 points for each correct answer   SCORE: _____

III. REFERENCE

Place the letter (a, b, c, d or e) of the correct answer in the space provided.

a. museum   **c.** encyclopedia
b. travel agent   **d.** calligrapher
                    e. library index card

_____ **1.** Where would you go to learn more about Tung's life?

_____ **2.** Where would you go to see Chinese paintings?

_____ **3.** Where would you go to arrange for a visit to China?

_____ **4.** Whom would you see to learn about Chinese letters?

_____ **5.** Where would you go to get a general overview on Chinese painting?

10 points for each correct answer   SCORE: _____

PERFECT TOTAL SCORE: 100   TOTAL SCORE: _____

IV. QUESTIONS FOR THOUGHT

What are the qualities you admire most about Tung? In what ways might you learn from them?

White-Water High

Jean George

The river is blue-green glass, and the sun warms my back. I am on a 22-foot (7-meter) raft with my daughter, Twig. Two guides and five other passengers are with us. In life jackets and rain pants, we sit sidesaddle, feet in on the raft rim. We are paddling down the New River, a deep waterway that cuts through the postcard-blue mountains of West Virginia. I hear a low drum roll up ahead. It is the Keeney Brothers, perhaps the longest and most powerful of all the rapids east of the Mississippi.

Twig and I are enjoying one of the fastest-growing sports in America today—river rafting. On this day, we have bounced down several smaller rapids while our guides told tales about the valley and the Keeneys, named for one of the area's first families. An hour ago we stopped for lunch on a rocky outcrop. Now we are back on the river with its fast water, and the drumming has become a throaty roar.

"Okay, gang," shouts John Dragan, our trip leader. "We're entering the good stuff."

Rapids are rated on a scale of one to six. A one is a beginner rapid; a six is for experts. Normally, the three Keeneys are rated as class five. "The water is high," says Dragan. "Today the Keeney Brothers are sixes."

I look behind me at Sara Corrie, 61, who says that she rafts "for survival." By this, she seems to mean just for the joy of it. She is experienced and sits low in the raft, ready for the good stuff just ahead.

Before setting off, we were given instructions in safety rules and also taught paddling strokes—forward, backward and sideways (or "draw"). We were told that when we hit fast water, we must paddle to a fast rhythm to get the boat moving faster than the river. "Only then can the raft be steered," Dragan told us. "And in the Keeneys every inch counts."

At the first rapids, the river narrows to a width of about 100 feet (30 meters). Thundering waves send spray 40 feet (12 meters) into the air. "Okay, gang," booms Dragan. "We'll enter to the left of that boulder. Does anyone want to walk around?" he asks.

The shore looks firm and steady, but no one answers.

"Fine! A good crew!" he exclaims, then says, "Now, brace yourselves against the knee behind you and the foot of the paddler across from you."

I look across at Dr. Paul Kanfer. He is a medical adviser who once a year gives a course to the guides in emergency medicine—everything from heart attacks to heat problems. Kanfer nods and we brace feet.

The first Keeney seems to shake the very mountain. The trip leader guides us through the storm by "reading the water." A V pointing downstream is a good path between two underwater rocks. The guides also watch for boiling, dangerous water. Finally, the leader judges the height of waves to determine how far below the surface lie the rocks that they mark.

We slide onto a green patch of water and are sucked into the main current. *"Draw* left! *Paddle* ahead on the right!" he shouts. "Right" means Twig, Mrs. Corrie and me. We are into the white water, and we dig in hard.

"Move it!" comes the call. *"Move* it. *Move* it."

Thunder rumbles over and under us. Waves break over our faces and shoulders. We slide down a jagged mountain of water, then up a tower of foam, balance an instant, then

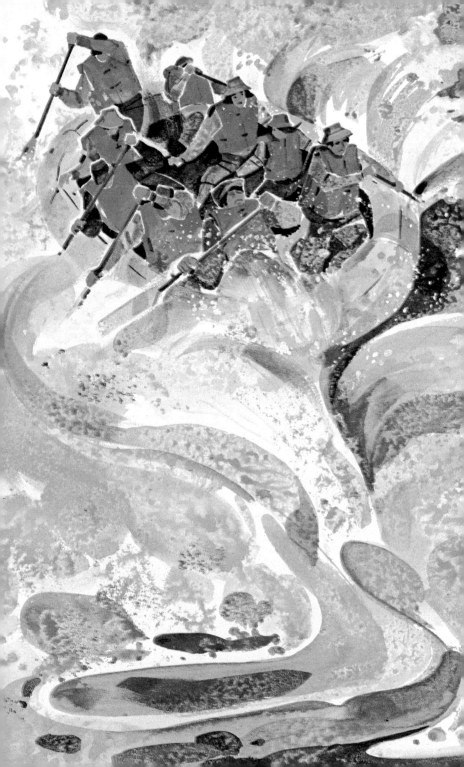

fall off the other side. A shout comes from my throat.

"Great!" shouts Dragan. "Now for Middle Keeney. Check your life jackets!"

We look at the buckles on our jackets, turn and check those of the person behind. The waves are more than 12 feet (4 meters) high. The water bubbles as we swing into position above the thundering rapids.

"Move it. Move it!" The call explodes. We pass a huge camelback rock, and I look down into Middle Keeney gorge. We ride, up, up, up, toss like a chip to the top of the crest, then drop into a hole. Rocks clink and roll as they scrape the bottom, and I realize we are deep into the riverbed.

Suddenly we bounce up and seesaw into a stretch of calm water. "Take five!" says Dragan.

I am soaked to the skin but warm with excitement. I rest, bail and listen to the water speak of rocks and millions of years of time. (The New River, the oldest on this continent, was new only to the pioneer rivermen who first saw it.)

This sport of rafting got its start at the close of World War II, when large surplus life rafts came on the market. One early rafter was an Oakland, California, printer named Lou Elliott. Lou floated his $30 rubber tub down the Colorado and the Rogue in Oregon. In 1963 he sold his print shop and gave full time to rafting people into the wilderness. A new industry was born. "In rafting," says Lou, "I find wonders I never knew existed."

In the United States today, there are more than 125 professional outfitters running river trips. Because of the various water ways, these trips are of many different types. On the upper Snake in Wyoming's Grand Teton National Park— the most rafted river in the world—the guides handle the raft while the people watch moose, bald eagles and snow-capped mountain peaks. On other trips, passengers control the raft while the guides paddle kayaks alongside. Many think our type, with guides and passengers rafting together, is the most fun. Trip costs vary from $5 to $10 for two to three hours on calm rivers, to about $40 a day per person for the heavy water.

The rest is over. We are soon moving to Lower Keeney. Dragan shouts, "Now for the prize! This rapid must be taken straight. Let's go!"

With a sucking snarl, Lower Keeney grabs us and starts sliding us from side to side. A chain of dark rocks is directly ahead. *"Draw right! Paddle ahead on the left!"* I pull on the oar for my life.

The current clutches. A sudden burst of power comes from all of us. We skim safely around the rocks and drop into a huge hole. We ride up, and I look down a waterfall that plunges 20 feet (6 meters) into white, boiling water. The river pushes us toward it, but we fight madly. At the brink, the raft obeys our strokes and takes us through the mid-channel.

"Perfect!" yells Dragan. Shouting and laughing, we ride the long stretch of water to the end of the run. A sense of wholeness binds our raft team, and we raise a cheer. Kanfer says, "We have been through the wilderness without leaving a single footmark." Sara Corrie laughs excitedly. "Yes," she agrees, then says, "We are wiser than we were at dawn."

Number of Words: 1169 ÷ _____ Minutes Reading Time = Rate _____

I. MAIN IDEA

Check ✓ the one statement which best describes what the story is about.

_____ **1.** Rafting on the New River in West Virginia is very different from rafting on the Snake River in Wyoming.

_____ **2.** The selection contains tips on river rafting, and how to avoid rapids that too many other people use.

_____ **3.** The author's experiences are a good example of why rafting is one of the fastest-growing sports today.

20 points for correct answer   SCORE: _____

II. OUTLINING

One part of this selection is outlined below. Some lines are blank. Write the item that best fits in each blank.

a. White-Water Rafting
b. Reaching a stretch of calm water

c. History of rafting
d. "Reading the water"

I. _____

    A.   Rafting on New River

        1. _____

        2. Waves 3.7 meters (over 3 feet) high in middle Keeney.

        3. _____

    B. _____

        1. Started at the close of WW II

        2. Lou Elliott, early rafter

10 points for each correct answer   SCORE: _____

III. PROBLEM SOLVING

How can rafting accidents be avoided? Write the letter of the item choice (a, b or c) that best completes each statement below.

_____ 1. Before going rafting over a rapid, find out
      a. the safest route to travel.
      b. how much rain fell near the river the night before.
      c. how it is rated by experienced rafters on a scale of 1 to 6.

_____ 2. Before setting off on a rafting trip, make sure
      a. you carry enough food and water for three days.
      b. everyone knows the safety rules and the paddling strokes.
      c. your raft's motor is working properly.

_____ 3. If a rapid looks too dangerous, you should
      a. get out and walk the raft around the rapid.
      b. tie two or three rafts together to make them float better.
      c. head for it at full speed.

_____ 4. When the raft hits fast water, you should
      a. slow down by back-paddling.
      b. get the boat moving faster than the river.
      c. let the current take control.

10 points for each correct answer   SCORE: _____

PERFECT TOTAL SCORE: 100   TOTAL SCORE: _____

IV. QUESTIONS FOR THOUGHT

What has this story taught you about white-water rafting? Would you like to try it? Explain your answer.

A SPANISH GHOST STORY

Ralph S. Boggs and Mary G. Davis

In the wide plain not far from the city of Toledo, Spain, there once stood a great gray castle. For many years before this story begins, no one had lived there because the castle was haunted. There was no living soul within its walls. And yet, on almost every night in the year, a thin, sad voice moaned, wept and wailed through the huge empty rooms. On All Hallows' Eve a ghostly light appeared in the chimney, a light that flared and died and flared again against the dark sky.

Learned doctors and brave adventurers had tried to banish the ghost. But each had been found in the great hall of the castle, sitting lifeless before the empty fireplace.

One day in late October, there came to the little village that nestled around the castle walls a brave and jolly tinker whose name was Esteban. And while he sat in the marketplace mending the pots and pans, the good wives told him about the haunted castle. It was All Hallows' Eve, they said, and if he would wait until nightfall, he could see the strange light flare up from the chimney. He might, if he dared go near enough, hear the thin, sad voice echo through the silent rooms.

"If I dare!" Esteban repeated scornfully. "You must know, good wives, that I—Esteban—fear nothing, neither ghost nor human. I will gladly sleep in the castle tonight and keep this dismal spirit company."

The good wives looked at him in amazement. Did Esteban know that if he succeeded in banishing the ghost, the owner of the castle would give him a thousand gold *reales*?

Esteban chuckled. If that was how matters stood, he would go to the castle at nightfall and do his best to get rid of the thing that haunted it. But he was a man who liked plenty to eat and drink and a fire to keep him company. They must bring to him a load of firewood, a side of bacon, a flask of wine, a dozen fresh eggs and a frying pan. This the good wives gladly did. As dusk fell, Esteban loaded these things on the donkey's back and set out for the castle. And you may be very sure that not one of the village people went very far along the way with him!

It was a dark night with a chill wind blowing and a hint of rain in the air. Esteban unsaddled his donkey and set him to graze on the short grass of the deserted courtyard. Then he carried his food and his firewood into the great hall. It was dark as pitch there. Bats beat their soft wings in his face, and the air felt cold and musty. He lost no time in piling some of his sticks in one corner of the huge stone fireplace and lighting them. As the red and golden flames leaped up the chimney, Esteban rubbed his hands. Then he settled himself comfortably on the hearth.

"*That* is the thing to keep off both cold and fear," he said.

Carefully slicing some bacon, he laid it in the pan and set it over the flames. How good it smelled! And how cheerful the sound of its crisp sizzling!

He had just lifted his flask to take a deep drink of the good wine, when down the chimney there came a thin, sad voice. "*Oh, me! Oh, me! Oh, me!*"

Esteban swallowed the wine and set the flask carefully down beside him.

"Not a very cheerful greeting, my friend," he said, as he moved the bacon on the pan so that it should be equally brown in all its parts. "But bearable to a man who is used to the braying of his donkey."

"*Oh, me!*" sobbed the voice. "*Oh, me! Oh, me!*"

Esteban lifted the bacon carefully from the hot fat and

laid it on a bit of brown paper to drain. Then he broke an egg into the frying pan. As he gently shook the pan so that the edges of his egg should be crisp and brown and the yolk soft and loose, the voice came again. Only this time it was shrill and frightened.

"Look out be-l-o-w-w-w. I'm f-a-l-l-i-n-g!"

"All right, answered Esteban. "Only don't fall into the frying pan."

With that, there was a thump, and on the hearth lay a man's leg! It was a good enough leg, and it was clothed in half of a pair of brown corduroy trousers.

Esteban ate his egg and a piece of bacon and drank again

from the flask of wine. The wind howled around the castle, and the rain beat against the windows.

Then, *"Look out below,"* called the voice sharply. *"I'm falling!"*

There was a thump, and on the hearth there lay a second leg, just like the first!

Esteban moved it away from the fire and piled on more sticks. Then he warmed the fat in the frying pan and broke into it a second egg.

"Look out below!" roared the voice. And now it was no longer thin, but strong and lusty. *"Look out below! I'm falling!"*

"Fall away," Esteban answered cheerfully. "Only don't spill my egg."

There was a thump, heavier than the first two, and on the hearth there lay a body. It was clothed in a blue shirt and a brown corduroy coat.

Esteban was eating his third egg and the last of the cooked bacon when the voice called again, and down fell first one arm and then the other.

"Now," thought Esteban, as he put the frying pan on the fire and began to cook more bacon. "Now there is only the head. I confess that I am rather curious to see the head."

"Look out below!" thundered the voice. "I'm falling—falling!"

And down the chimney there came tumbling a head!

It was a good enough head, with thick black hair, a long black beard, and dark eyes that looked a little strained and anxious. Esteban's bacon was only half cooked. Nevertheless, he removed the pan from the fire and laid it on the hearth. And it is a good thing that he did, because before his eyes the parts of the body joined together, and a living man—or his ghost—stood before him! That was a sight that might have startled Esteban into burning his fingers with the bacon fat.

"Good evening," said Esteban. "Will you have an egg and a bit of bacon?"

"No, I want no food," the ghost answered. "But I will tell you this, right here and now. You are the only man, out of all those who have come to the castle, to stay here until I could get my body together again. The others died of sheer fright before I was half finished."

"That is because they did not have sense enough to bring food and fire with them," Esteban replied coolly. And he turned back to his frying pan.

"Wait a minute!" pleaded the ghost. "If you will help me a bit more, you will save my soul and get me into the Kingdom of Heaven. Out in the courtyard, under a cypress tree, there are buried three bags—one of copper coins, one of silver coins and one of gold coins. I stole them from some thieves and brought them here to the castle to hide. But no sooner did I have them buried, than the thieves overtook me, murdered me and cut my body into pieces. But they did not find the coins. Now, you come with me and dig them up. Give the copper coins to the Church, the silver coins to the poor, and keep the gold coins for yourself. Then I will have paid for my sins and can go to the Kingdom of Heaven."

This suited Esteban. So he went out into the courtyard with the ghost. And you should have heard how the donkey brayed when he saw them!

When they reached the cypress tree in a corner of the courtyard, the ghost commanded Esteban to dig.

"Dig yourself," answered Esteban.

So the ghost dug, and after a time the three bags of money appeared.

Esteban carried the coins into the great hall of the castle, fried and ate another egg and then went peacefully to sleep before the fire.

The next morning when the village people came to carry away Esteban's body, they found him making an omelette out of the last of the fresh eggs.

"Are you alive?" they gasped, blinking in disbelief.

"I am," Esteban answered. "And the food and the firewood lasted through very nicely. Now I will go to the owner of the castle and collect my thousand gold *reales*. The ghost has gone for good. You will find his clothes lying out in the courtyard."

Before their astonished eyes, Esteban loaded the bags of coins on the donkey's back and left.

First he collected the thousand gold *reales* from the grateful lord of the castle. Then he returned to Toledo, gave the copper coins to the pastor of his church and, true to his promise, gave out the silver ones to the poor. On the thousand *reales* and the golden coins, he lived in ease and contentment for many years.

"Now, will you promise to do just what I asked you to do?" asked the ghost.

"Yes, I promise," Esteban answered.

"Then," said the ghost, "Strip my garments from me."

This Esteban did, and instantly the ghost disappeared, leaving its clothes lying there on the short grass of the courtyard. It went straight up to Heaven and knocked on the Gate. St. Peter opened it and, when the spirit explained that he had paid for his sins, gave him a warm welcome.

Number of Words: 1639 ÷ _____ Minutes Reading Time = Rate _____

I. STORY ELEMENTS

The readers' feelings are supposed to change as they go through the story. Check ✓ 5 statements below which explain how the authors play on reader emotions.

_____ **1.** The authors describe the castle to create a scary feeling.

_____ **2.** They show how dangerous the castle has been in the past.

_____ **3.** They describe their own experiences in the castle.

_____ **4.** They describe the villagers' scared reaction to Esteban's plan.

_____ **5.** They show us Esteban being unconcerned about the goings-on in the chimney.

_____ **6.** They quote Esteban's humorous replies to the ghost.

_____ **7.** They made the ghost appear dull and foolish.

8 points for each correct answer   SCORE: _____

II. CHARACTERIZATION

What does the story reveal about Esteban? Check ✓ five statements that correctly describe him.

_____ **1.** He is greedy and would do anything for money.

_____ **2.** He has a lot of common sense and does not believe wild tales.

_____ **3.** He does not scare easily and is not afraid of ghosts.

_____ **4.** He is calm and patient and does not get easily ruffled.

_____ **5.** He has a sense of humor, even when talking to a ghost.

_____ **6.** He keeps his promises and is as good as his word.

_____ **7.** He always manages to get his way with other people.

6 points for each correct answer   SCORE: _____

III. CAUSE/EFFECT

Each event in column A caused an effect listed in column B. Match each effect with its cause. Write the letter of your choice in space provided.

	A		B
_____ **1.**	People dared Esteban to go near the castle.	**a.**	He calmly kept on cooking his food.
_____ **2.**	Esteban wanted to feel warm and safe.	**b.**	He took off the ghost's clothes.
_____ **3.**	Esteban wanted to show the ghost he was not afraid.	**c.**	He lit a fire in the fireplace.
_____ **4.**	Esteban was not scared by the falling leg.	**d.**	He decided to spend the night with the ghost.
_____ **5.**	Esteban wanted to help the ghost get to Heaven.	**e.**	He ate the egg and bacon and drank some wine.

6 points for each correct answer   SCORE: _____

PERFECT TOTAL SCORE: 100   TOTAL SCORE: _____

IV. QUESTION FOR THOUGHT

Have you ever accepted a challenge like Esteban did? Describe it if you have faced a challenge, or make up one if you have not had to face a real challenge. Tell how you would meet it.

Magnificent Marathon

Sheila Cragg

It used to be that when young Patty Wilson ran, her arms and legs flailed like a rag doll's. She was awkward, uncoordinated. She couldn't even throw a ball.

Many children are clumsy, but Patty felt her ineptness more deeply than other children. She came from a family of athletes, a concentrated world of sports and competition. "I felt left out," she says. Timidly, she began to run a mile with her father, Jim. He was always at her side, watching. For not only did Patty lack athletic ability, she had epilepsy.

Her first modest achievement came at age 13 when she ran the 30 miles (48 kilometers) from her home in La Palma, California, to her grandparents' home in Los Angeles. In her mind were thoughts of Pete Strudwick, a marathoner she'd met just before she began running. Like him, she was fiercely determined to overcome an obstacle. Pete runs on stumps because he has no feet.

In 1975 Patty and her dad ran the 100 miles (161 kilometers) from La Palma to San Diego. Her determination seemed unshatterable.

But she was to have a moment of truth. That year, as a high-school freshman, Patty joined the all-male cross-country team. During her very first meet, Patty had her first complex partial seizure. It was 90° Fahrenheit (32° Celsius) and smoggy. A quarter-mile out, she began running like a mechanical tin soldier. Somehow she finished the race standing, but she remembered nothing about the event.

A complex partial seizure is one form of epilepsy: confusion, a blank stare, robot-like movements. There would be more seizures, but Patty's doctor felt that she could continue running—if someone were always with her.

A fiercely determined Patty Wilson enjoying a cross country run with older competitors

Her father, Jim, is always at Patty's side during workouts, watching.

Patty was invited to the Santa Barbara Cross-Country Invitational for high-school girls. "I was scared," she says. "It was a 2-mile (3-kilometer) race over hilly terrain I'd never seen." She won, nevertheless, and her team voted her Most Inspirational Runner.

Her next test came a few weeks later, when she and her dad ran 300 miles (483 kilometers) to Las Vegas. After the school year, they ran a grueling 508 miles (818 kilometers) to San Francisco.

In 1976-77 Patty, then a sophomore, competed on the boys' cross-country and the girls' track teams, and Jim started talking about a 1000-mile (1609-kilometer) run from Buena Park, California, to Portland, Oregon. "I was opposed," says Patty's mother, Dotty. But Patty and Jim persuaded Dotty, who is a nurse, to help them in their greatest challenge.

To train for this daring marathon, Patty and her dad ran 125 miles (201 kilometers) a week. During one session, Jim burst ahead of her up a hill. He ran a quarter of a mile and turned to check on Patty. She was nowhere in sight.

Jim ran a mile east, then a mile west. It was twilight as he retraced their route. No one had seen Patty. "I panicked!" Jim recalls. "I was afraid she'd been hit by a car."

He ran home, and in the darkness he and Dotty drove the streets searching. When Patty finally turned up at home, confused, Jim realized that she had had another seizure.

After this frightening episode, Jim watched Patty more closely when they ran. She didn't let it bother her.

Patty's high-school coaches had known about her epilepsy. She talked freely about it. But up to this point, her parents had kept it a secret from the press and public.

"Patty's first seizure occurred in the third grade," Dotty recalls. "The children began to avoid Patty after that, and she didn't want to return to school. I figured that's the way the general public would react. We didn't even tell her grandparents for a long time."

"I was scared of the word epilepsy," Jim says. "I didn't know what it was. When I began to understand, it didn't frighten me as much. Her epilepsy is mild, but she does have it. So, we thought, why not help those less fortunate than we are?" That decision led to the Wilsons' public announcement, a month before the Portland run, that Patty had epilepsy.

In June 1977 television crews, reporters, state, county and city officials, epilepsy-society members and well-wishers gathered to send Patty off. She radiated warmth, moving among the crowd, laughing and talking. Then she was off, almost lost among the runners who had come to accompany her for a way.

Relaxing with her athletic family, Patty, bottom center, is surrounded clockwise by Richard, Sandy, Jim and Dotty.

Within 25 miles (40 kilometers), Patty faced her first challenge, one that would have stopped many athletes. She suffered a stress fracture in the third metatarsal bone of her left foot. Jim and Dotty took her to a hospital. The doctor who X-rayed her foot advised that it be put in a cast for six weeks. If she continued, he warned, she might never be able to run in a race again.

"It was my decision to go on," claims Patty. "It was a challenge to see how strong I could be within myself." She also seemed to sense how much she symbolized to others.

Patty's second challenge occurred when the Wilsons realized that the run would take two weeks longer than anticipated. They had chosen a coastal route for its cooler temperatures. "But we didn't figure it would be more than 300 miles (483 kilometers) farther going up the coast and over," says Dotty.

At first, Patty didn't think the extra distance would bother her. Then she'd wake up every morning and think, "I can't make it—1310 miles (2108 kilometers)! Dad helped me think in terms of running mile by mile, day by day. That relieved me from dwelling on the awesome distance."

A small recreational vehicle was the Wilsons' home away from home. They rose every morning at 4:30, and Patty would begin her painful preparations. Her mother had to drain a score of blisters on Patty's feet. (This had to be repeated every afternoon and evening.) Her father wrapped Patty's feet and her legs from thigh to calf.

They were on the road and running by 6 o'clock, averaging 31 miles (50 kilometers) a day. "Patty pulled me along, and I pulled her along," Jim recalls. "We told each other stories, played games and collected returnable bottles. Patty practiced her Spanish or imitated her favorite star, Barbra Streisand. The camper, driven ahead by Dotty, was our incentive. Just reach it! When we were in pain and discouraged, we told each other to bite the bullet."

After 10 to 15 miles (16 to 24 kilometers), the runners would stop and drink juice. During the day they consumed about 2 gallons (7.6 liters) of fruit juice and a special drink designed to restore the body's potassium and electrolyte balance. They also took salt tablets. Breakfast and dinner were their only solid meals.

Patty's left foot was so swollen that it barely fit in her sneaker. They tried ice packs, hot soaks and different shoes. Along with three drugs to control her epilepsy, Patty took pain medication. Twenty-one days out, in the middle of the night, she became violently ill.

But the next morning, Patty struggled through 3 miles (5 kilometers). She slept for five hours, then ran 15 more miles (24 kilometers). Her steely mental fiber kept her running long after her body cried quits.

Hills and head winds were another problem. "It always seemed as if the biggest hill was at the end of the day's run," says Jim. "If we'd consulted cyclists, we would have run from Portland to Los Angeles, instead of the other way round."

If Mother Nature was bad, human nature was often worse. From passing cars hecklers yelled, "Is that as fast as you can go?" Once, children bombed them with dirt clods.

From the Oregon border on, high-school track teams ran with Patty. And, all the way,

Joined by Gov. Straub in final mile, Patty is triumphant as she is applauded by spectators in Buena Park, California to Portland, Oregon run.

A living inspiration for others
to overcome adversity

During the final leg into Portland, crowds poured out to greet them. Governor Bob Straub, a regular jogger, joined Patty for the final mile. In the last 100 yards (91 meters), her father looked over to see if Patty had a smile of victory, but she could only grimace from the incredible pain.

Then it was over. They were swooped up in welcoming ceremonies. There were some in the crowd who fought back tears, others who wept openly. Straub proclaimed July 29 Patty Wilson Day throughout Oregon. It was a special day for everyone who had ever struggled against adversity, and especially for those labeled "handicapped."

"I haven't been stopped because of epilepsy. I never will be!" Patty said after the run. "Now, maybe others with a handicap will be encouraged to try something they've wanted to do."

people with epilepsy stopped and talked with her. "They didn't care about the running. They cared that Patty carried the message that she had epilepsy," her father says. "She was a light for them."

Number of Words: 1487 ÷ _____ Minutes Reading Time = Rate _____

I. MAIN IDEA

Check √ the one statement which best describes what the story is about.

_____ **1.** Governor Straub (of Oregon) declares July 28 Patty Wilson Day.

_____ **2.** Patty Wilson became a successful long-distance runner in spite of her epilepsy.

_____ **3.** Patty Wilson met great hardship during the long marathon.

10 points for correct answer   SCORE: _____

II. PROBLEM SOLVING

Long-distance running can cause many physical problems. Circle the letter of the item (a, b or c) that best completes each statement below.

1. To be in shape for a marathon race, a runner must
    a. run about 15 to 20 miles a day.
    b. rest up for a week before the race.
    c. eat very little.
2. During a race, a runner needs to
    a. eat something every few miles.
    b. drink plenty of fluids.
    c. think about the other runners.
3. To avoid blisters, a runner should
    a. change his shoes often.
    b. wear heavy socks or wrappings around his feet.
    c. soak his feet in cold water.

10 points for each correct answer   SCORE: _____

III. VOCABULARY

Write the letter of the word or phrase that means the same as the word in italics.

_____ 1. When Patty was very small, she showed *ineptness* at sports; but her will-power and training helped her run a long marathon.
   a. talent   **b.** lack of ability   **c.** promise

_____ 2. A long hike in the hot sun is *grueling;* it is relaxing and comfortable to hike on a cool day.
   a. fun and exciting   **b.** carefree and bracing
   c. harsh and exhausting

_____ 3. Some people *radiate* warmth; while others show little feeling.
   a. glow with   **b.** show their tempers   **c.** hold back

10 points for each correct answer   SCORE: _____

IV. GENERALIZATIONS

Check √ *three statements below that are generally true about long distance running.*

_____ 1. Anybody can become a marathon runner.

_____ 2. Long-distance running is suitable for both men and women.

_____ 3. Long-distance running is not as tough as football.

_____ 4. It takes courage to run day after day, as Patty did.

10 points for each correct answer   SCORE: _____

PERFECT TOTAL SCORE: 100   TOTAL SCORE _____

V. QUESTION FOR THOUGHT

How might the example set by Patty Wilson encourage you?

Trouble At Churchill

Richard C. Davids

At the Churchill Legion Hall, a bear walks in at midday and ambles toward a crowd of dart throwers. Suddenly, the club steward, an old British army major, shouts, "You're no member. Get out!" The bear leaves.

When an airline agent and his family sit down to dinner in their summer cabin, a bear leaps through the window and starts helping itself at the family table. No one attempts to stop the intruder.

The trouble at Churchill is that, for several months starting in September, polar bears walk the streets any hour of the day or night. Often they are followed by a crowd of children, dogs and picture takers, taxing the efforts of Canadian Mounties and conservation officers to keep bears and people a safe distance apart. The task would be easier except that no one wants to shoot the polar bears. They are far too valuable. There may be no more than 12,000 of the splendid animals left in the world.

Polar bear travels past observation tower containing patrol scouts.

WHY CHURCHILL?

Churchill is a central Canadian village of 1600. It is the end of the line for a railroad bringing wheat from the Canadian prairies to be loaded on ships for Europe. It is also the end of the line for an age-old migration of polar bears which, every summer, follows the coast north for 200 miles (322 kilometers) to Cape Churchill, 40 miles (65 kilometers) east of town, where the big males wait for winter. Young bears and females with cubs are pushed on westward along the water's edge into town.

This is hard to believe: a town on the travel path of what many naturalists believe to be the most dangerous meat-eater in North America.

Nowhere else are so many polar bears found in one place. In winter, bears strike out north and east over the ice for 95 miles (150 kilometers) or more to hunt. But constant north winds and current move broken pack ice south, and along with it the bears. In summer, the last of the melting ice hangs up on the shallow flats on the southwest rim of the bay. So here, in July, the bears are forced ashore. A few move inland, but most follow the coast. Ice—which means bears can start hunting again—forms two and even three weeks earlier at Churchill.

GRIN AND BEAR IT

There was a bear at the Churchill airport last October when photographer Dan Guravich and I flew in. As we rode in the bear patrol truck with Roy Bukowsky, a conservation officer, the radio crackled to warn of another bear in town that morning. Asleep beside a building, the beautiful, snow-white animal looked no more dangerous than a child's over-sized toy. But it was chased away with something that looked like a giant firecracker.

The next morning, a trap, one block from our hotel, held a young bear that was calmed, measured and flown out of town.

The following night, the Mounties answered a bear call. When they came to the last house on the street, it was a bear that had come to the window to look out. Routed with noisemakers, it played hide-and-seek for the next half-hour and finally hid inside an abandoned bus.

Later, as we watched 25 big males at the Cape from a 40-foot (12-meter) tower, they seemed more bored than hungry, sleeping or strolling through flocks of willow ptarmigan. Two spent the day wrestling, mock fighting and resting. Only when the helicopter with its tagging crew came near did they hurry away. There were bears loafing everywhere along the coast. From a plane we saw 67 beautiful animals in one hour resting in the willows just back of high water or curled asleep in beds of kelp.

BACKYARD BEARS

Until recently, polar bears were creatures of mystery, known only to Eskimos and explorers traveling vast expanses by dogsled and snowshoes. But at Churchill, bears literally come to the doorstep of researchers. The results of research studies have helped the people of Churchill live with the bears.

Principal researchers at Churchill are Dr. Charles J. Jonkel of the University of Montana, but formerly with the Canadian Wildlife Service; Dr. Ian Stirling of the Canadian Wildlife Service; and Dr. Nils Oritsland of the University of Oslo, Norway. Their graduate students, along with conservation officers under the direc-

tion of Dick Robertson, capture bears in snares or traps, ear-tag, tattoo, weigh, take blood samples, extract a small tooth (a cross section reveals age the way tree rings do) and paint bold numbers on their sides so they can be watched at a distance.

Ear-tagging studies indicate that polar bears are not nomads. Fifty-two bears were tagged in Churchill and transported south by plane. Almost half made the 250-mile (402-kilogram) return trek the following year, three within two weeks and a mother and her cubs in 18 days.

Bears are wonderfully prepared for their rugged life. Except for the worst blizzards, which they wait out in temporary dens in the snow, they come to life as the weather grows colder, sliding down snowbanks with great pleasure. A dense fur that feels like fleece covers them completely. Even the soles of the feet are densely set with hair. The fur covers a skin almost as black as their coal-colored noses. To keep the cold out, fat often 4 inches (102 millimeters) thick covers much of the body. Across the shoulders outside the fat layer, Dr. Oritsland discovered a thin sheet of muscle-

Polar bears "come to life as the weather grows colder" and seek temporary dens in the snow.

controlling blood vessels that open to let out heat when the bear is hot and that close in cold weather. A grown male is powerful enough to snatch up a 200-pound (90-kilogram) ringed seal with the ease of a cat catching a mouse or to kill a 500-pound (225-kilogram) bearded seal with a single blow of its 50-pound (20-kilogram) paw. And bears are swift. A young one was clocked galloping along a road at 35 miles per hour (55 kilometers per hour). They can swim 6 miles per hour (10 kilometers per hour) and can go nonstop for 100 miles (160 kilometers) or more.

Their sense of smell is legendary. Eskimos claim that bears can scent a seal 20 miles (32 kilometers) away. Roy Bukowsky's pickup with its lingering smell of bait is a magnet. Once he started out from his downtown office with a bear aboard.

Few mothers in nature are so devoted to their young. A polar bear will attack anything in her cubs' defense. In March when she introduces her blinking young to the bright outdoor world, she starts a trek to the sea, stopping often to let the cubs nurse and crawl on her back to warm their feet. Some-

Dens afford polar bears shelter from the Arctic weather.

times they ride on her back. In the water they may hitch a ride, clinging to her tail. Despite such care, the first few months are critical in the life of a cub. In order to learn more about this key time, biologists have searched for den areas.

When a party of trappers went inland by dogsled to hunt beaver along the Owl River in 1968, they saw bear tracks. Informed of the tracks, Dr. Jonkel visited the area by snowshoe. He thought he must be dreaming. Only 40 miles (64 kilometers) from Churchill, there were dens everywhere—in the snow, along stream banks and mounds of peat. Some were barely 10 feet apart. Flying over after every snowfall, he counted tracks from dens to the shore ice. In 1974 some 89 bears emerged with 168 cubs, making Owl River one of the biggest denning areas in the world.

Jonkel thinks that because there are so many bears at Churchill, their life-style is changing. Used to being alone, the bears are staying in groups more. It seems that they sometimes act as a community.

HOW DANGEROUS ARE POLAR BEARS?

With all their strength and splendid weapons of teeth and claws, bears are generally retiring. When they see a man for the first time, it is probably interest more than wanting to pick a fight that makes them draw closer. It is something else when a bear is angry. Annoyed by the barking of the only remaining team of huskies in Eskimo Point, a bear recently killed each one.

In all, at Churchill there have been two mauling incidents and one death. All the bears involved were killed by the Mounties, and Dr. Jonkel's studies showed that the three bears had been bothered or hurt by humans. Nevertheless, bears do kill even if they have not been bothered by humans. Just after we left Churchill, an airport employee narrowly escaped death. Guiding a plane on the ground, he was puzzled that the pilot kept blinking his lights. By chance, the employee shone his flashlight over his shoulder and saw a bear charging, not 5 feet (1.5 meters) away. He ran toward the whirling propeller—it seemed a lesser danger—but slipped on ice

For all their strength and splended weapons of teeth and claws, bears are generally retiring.

just as the bear took a giant swipe at him. The pilot revved his motors and the bear, a mother with young, took off and rejoined her cubs.

SMART, CLUMSY, ENTERTAINING

Despite the very real dangers of polar bears, most Churchill residents wouldn't have it otherwise. Dr. Sharon Cohen of the Churchill clinic adds a word of explanation: "Nothing unites the people of the town as much as polar bears. We love them."

Resident Doug Weber says: "I only wish they'd go out the same hole they come in." His goose-hunting cabins were broken into six times in one winter. "It never fails," he says. "They make a new hole in the wall or window or door when they leave." If bears increase, and proposed control measures don't work, Weber favors limited hunting to make bears more wary. Some of his friends counter: How does a dead bear learn to be wary? Churchill is determined that bears and people coexist, and to that end there are slide shows and lectures at school. A bear patrol of students checks for the presence of bears before school dismisses. Phone directories list bear-alert numbers.

In 1977, in the first polar-bear tour, a dozen Americans flew along the coast in helicopters. The excitement over what they saw may prompt Canada to create one or more bear-watching towers expressly for tourists.

A few businessmen see a possibly good tourist trade building up. But, for the most part, Churchill simply likes its bears.

Number of Words: 2100 ÷ _____ Minutes Reading Time = Rate _____

An observation tower patrol person reports latest bear citings to headquarters.

I. SUMMARY

Check √ *two statements below that could be included in a short summary of the story.*

_____ **1.** The residents are determined that bears and people can co-exist; but life in Churchill can be full of surprises!

_____ **2.** Bears have been found in the most unusual places: the Legion Hall, the airport, an abandoned bus, a pickup truck.

_____ **3.** A limited hunting season has already been declared, to keep the number of bears down.

_____ **4.** Conducting research on polar bears in Churchill is easy, since they literally come to the researchers' doorstep.

5 points for each correct answer   SCORE: _____

II. SEQUENCE

The statements below describe the life cycle of the polar bear. Number them in order.

_____ **a.** When the ice breaks up, the bears are forced ashore.

_____ **b.** Every summer, they migrate north along the coast.

_____ **c.** In winter, they migrate north along the coast.

_____ **d.** The north winds and the currents push the ice pack south.

_____ **e.** By September, they have reached Churchill and the area around it.

8 points for each correct answer   SCORE: _____

III. SUPPORTING DETAILS

Circle the letter of the phrase that best completes each statement below.

1. Churchill is a Canadian town of
   a. 500 people.   **b.** 1600 people.   **c.** 5000 people.

2. When a polar bear gets too close, the people of Churchill
   a. chase it away with giant firecrackers.
   b. shoot and kill it.
   c. go into hiding.

3. Polar bears can survive the cold because of
   a. their habit of sleeping through the winter.
   b. their thick fur and a four-inch layer of fat.
   c. their constant migration.

4. Polar bears spend much of their time
   a. running.   **b.** traveling.   **c.** loafing.

5. One of the biggest denning areas in the world is
   a. at Eskimo Point.   **b.** along the Owl River.
   c. Antarctica.

---

8 points for each correct answer   SCORE: _____

PERFECT TOTAL SCORE: 100   TOTAL SCORE: _____

IV. QUESTIONS FOR THOUGHT

What would life in Churchill be like? What particular interests can you imagine yourself engaged in?

Nancy whacking a long drive
down the fairway

Burning Up the Links

Grace Lichtenstein

"They've got the wrong 'Wonder Woman' on TV," sports pros are saying. What they mean is that in less than a year, 21-year-old Nancy Lopez went from nobody to superstar, and joined the ranks of Billie Jean King, Chris Evert, Nadia Comaneci and Dorothy Hamill. Nancy had come along faster since turning pro than anyone in women's modern athletic history. Although it is unusual for a Mexican-American to star in a country-club sport like golf, it is not unheard of—Lee Trevino is the most famous example.

In her first year as a pro, Nancy won more than any other sister competitor; she captured seven tournaments, five big ones in a row. It was a new record for the women's tour. At the same time, she also broke the prize-money record for rookies in both the men's and women's tours. This made a big mark in the sports world, since there is more prize money in the pot on the men's tour.

Her fellow golfers have watched Nancy perform and have nothing but praise for her success. She has also dazzled the press. She has put Roswell, New Mexico, on the map as more than just the hometown of a singer named John Denver. Nancy has thrilled Mexican-Americans all over the country, and finally brought women's golf the headlines it has needed to hurl it into the front ranks of sports.

Every sport seems to need at least one star to bring in support money from television and sponsors. For women's golf, Nancy Lopez is that star,

Flashing some of the charm for which an unaffected Nancy Lopez has become famous

and she could not have come at a better time. Athletics are no longer considered a freak show or passing fad among American women. Athletics have become a sincere side interest and, in some cases, a true passion. Female players in sports such as tennis, college basketball and gymnastics are followed as seriously as males in the same games. But pro golf, which was among the very first sports to attract women in large numbers, has always lagged behind.

Nancy is all smiles and poise as her gallery of fans looks on.

NANCY IN PERSON

In person, on and off the fairway, Nancy is a complete charmer. Her teeth are suitable for toothpaste ads and her smile seems to stretch the width of the fairway. Her newly trimmed figure and stylish haircut have won the hearts and minds of males and females from 10 to 60 who line up for her autograph. They are won over by her poise on display throughout game competition.

The bigger and louder the gallery, the happier and more sure of herself Nancy is. She adores her father, who taught her to play golf, buys her older sister fur coats and cracks jokes when she's angry.

Other than that, she's a pretty everyday kid. In fact, the other pros call her "The Kid."

Like Chris Evert, who won Wimbledon laurels at 19, there is no question about what Nancy can do, even if she is young. She has as much warmth, liveliness and kindness in her personality as she does athletic talent. This blend doesn't happen very often. To describe her is to risk sounding like an adoring fan. But what can you say when the brightest new female light in sports tells you the fa-

mous person she'd most like to meet is John Travolta, and at the same time, you notice a religious book poking out of a corner of her suitcase?

Nearly two hours after she had won her fifth victory in a row, Nancy was still dazed from the pressure, the victory, the ceremony, the telephone calls and the press conference.

And when she stepped outside the clubhouse at Locust Hill, the newest idol of golf found 50 people, mainly children, still waiting eagerly for her autograph. Without a trace of impatience, she stood and signed every last one.

"I can't believe it. I never thought it would be like this," Nancy said. "A lot of people know who I am! I was always on the other side."

The "other side" was Roswell, a dusty unknown Southwest town of some 35,000 people. It is located in a region called Little Texas because of its closeness and similarity to the western part of the Lone Star State. The Lopez family moved there shortly after Nancy was born in Torrance, California, on Jan. 6, 1957.

Nancy's father, Domingo, a gentle man who is fond of company, loved the sport. He had his second daughter trailing him on the nine-hole city golf course by the age of seven.

The tale of how Nancy practiced with sawed-off golf clubs, how her father gave her the only lessons she's ever had, how both parents saved their pennies and struggled so the apple of Daddy's eye could get ahead with her game, is fast becoming part of golfing legend. Her brother-in-law, Bernie Guevara, says Nancy's parents would not let her wash dishes because her hands had to be protected. She herself says her mother gave up the chance to buy a dishwasher later on so that Nancy would have enough money for travel

An adoring father, Domingo Lopez, is rewarded as much by Nancy's kiss as her achievement on the golf links.

in the amateur golf circuit.

Nevertheless, it was not a poverty-to-riches story so much as an all-American one. Domingo Lopez came from a family of nine with a cotton farm in Valentine, in west Texas. Although he himself never got past the third grade, he learned auto mechanics and moved to Roswell because it offered a chance to earn a living there.

Mr. Lopez, who often comes to Nancy's tournaments, runs a successful auto body repair shop in Roswell.

A good-enough baseball pitcher and center fielder to be offered a tryout with a minor league team, Mr. Lopez turned it down because the money wasn't good enough to support his wife. "I feel if I had had the chance like Nancy, I could have made the big league," he said the other day, without bitterness.

At the age of 40 he discovered golf through a friend, and within a year and a half he was "pretty good." When his little daughter trailed after him on the golf course, he was willing to do anything to give her the chance he had missed.

How good was she as a child? "She would say, 'Daddy, would you rather have a son or me?' And I said, 'You,' " he recalled fondly. "After all, she was good enough to play on the boys' high school team."

In high school Nancy was, in her own words, "just a normal little person," active in swimming, basketball, track, gymnastics, Girl Scouts and a sorority called "Chums." She tore the ligaments in her left knee playing high-school flag football. That is why she has an athletic-looking scar that still shows. Her best friend was a Mexican-American, but more of her friends were Anglos.

Still, she felt some discrimination once in a while. "I dated a guy whose parents didn't like me because I was Mexican-American," Nancy says. However, many Anglos supported her early career by bringing their business to her father. A few, especially those at the more select country clubs, now pretend to be old friends, although once they would have little to do with the family.

By her early teens, Nancy was making a name for herself in amateur golf. "I had heard all about her when she was 14," says another pro golfer, Jane Blalock. "She could outhit me then." Nancy's father managed to keep her going without a sponsor. He was ready to mortgage his house or sell his business if he needed money to support her career. "She never wanted to use my money," he says. After winning almost every amateur tournament, Nancy accepted an athletic scholarship to the University of Tulsa, but she quit college to turn professional.

Nancy had already played her first U.S. Women's Open as an amateur at 16. "I felt like I had no other place to go. I needed to go forward and set other goals, reach the highest

Fully aware of and prepared for the hard road of professional golf, Nancy responds to the challenge with determination.

point of my whole career. I knew it wasn't glamorous, that it was a lot of hard work and a lot of traveling," she says.

soon as she won the first one, she relaxed." The remarkable golfing career of Nancy Lopez had begun.

THE PAYOFF

Nancy's long experience as an amateur, the fact that she, rather than her father, made the choice to turn pro, plus her remarkable skills began to pay off right away. Her first event as a pro was the 1977 U.S. Women's Open. She finished as runner-up. She came in second in her next two tournaments as well, before leaving the tour to get over a small injury to her hand.

That summer, her mother died suddenly. Nancy quit the tour for a few weeks and vowed to win her first tournament as a tribute to her mother. "I was more ready to win after she passed away," she says quietly. (The comment suggests a special quality of winning athletes—the ability to turn the worst tragedy into a reason for trying harder.) Her first victory came in Florida. Her father thinks it actually might have happened sooner. "Nancy tried too hard for Momma," he says. "As long as you try too hard in any sport you aren't going to win. As

A CLOSEUP

Several factors explain why Nancy is special on the golf course. She has a strange swing, a deadly putting game and a "go-for-it" attitude. Her coolness in tight spots hides a basically emotional nature—a nature that shows only at certain times, as when she hit a spectator with a ball.

The morning had started early. After a light breakfast, Nancy became all business as she worked steadily alongside her opponents. Teeing off at the 10th hole, she struck the spectator.

As she rushed up to him, tears welling up in Nancy's walnut brown eyes, the injured man mumbled to a friend kneeling beside him, "At least I'll get to meet her now."

By her own account, the 21-year-old Miss Lopez was so "shook-up" by the accident, that she couldn't keep her mind on the game. She made a big mistake and then another one.

Only after she had made up her mind to dedicate the tournament to the hard-headed

spectator did she truly steady-herself. In the next two days, with pressure on her shoulders that even some World Series veterans would bow under, Nancy sent the huge groups following her into waves of happiness, on her way to winning her fifth tournament in a row.

That night, after dinner with Dick Schaap, the writer who was already lined up to do her biography, Nancy tried to unwind by spending some time at a disco across from the motel. All it did was get her to bed

late. The next day she was tired and the air was damp, and both took their toll. On the 18th green, she made a big mistake. Her eyes got smaller as she strode into the scorekeeper's tent, still behind the leader Jane Blalock.

"If I weren't here I'd be cussin'," she said with a rather

The serious business of winning a tournament frequently gives way to the Lopez charm, as Nancy anticipates the outcome of her latest line drive.

fierce smile as she walked into the pressroom. "I'm mad, I'm hot." She had worked on her putting for three years. Miss Blalock and others feel that Nancy Lopez is "the best putter, male or female, in the game today." As it turned out, that "mistake" Nancy made in a weird way may have won her the tournament.

At the time of that fifth tournament, Jane Blalock, a $102,000 winner the year before, was enjoying the top position. She had to say that it was a bit "scary" to have a streaking player like Nancy behind her. But she had made up her mind not to think about it.

"We all said, 'Let's win one. Let's one of us knock her off this week,' because it's a challenge," Jane Blalock said of Nancy. "But it's amazed me. There hasn't been any jealousy that can be seen. I think maybe the girls are all smart enough to realize how much she's doing for all of us."

As Carol Mann, a spokesperson for the pros, noted, it is hateful to compare pros. Yet golf followers are already comparing the impact of Miss Lopez on the women's game with that of Arnold Palmer on the men's game 20 years before. Further, Jane Blalock, whom

As to why Nancy Lopez golfs: "I feel as if I'm making people believe in a lot of things."

Nancy streaked past to win in that fifth tournament, calls her "a Nicklaus in golf ability." And he is thought to be the greatest modern golfer.

"There hasn't been a Nancy Lopez before. No one even close," Miss Blalock adds. "She has the appeal of Palmer and the charm of Trevino," marvels Ray Volpe, commissioner of the Ladies' Professional Golf Association.

Jane Blalock's feelings were seconded by every player I spoke with. Even before the rash of publicity, Nancy Lopez was well liked by the other golfers on the tour.

She tends to keep to herself, except for outings now and then with friends, such as Jo

Away from the tension of tournament golf, Nancy's relaxation comes from simply enjoying life.

Ann Washam. However, she is a good partner on the course, and the pros have made note of her maturity. Kathy Whitworth, at 38 the all-time money winner on the tour (about $750,000), noted, "She's on a tidal wave and I'm excited for her." To Carol Mann, Nancy Lopez had brought the tour an incredible amount of atten-tion. "She's a charming girl and her personality really comes across. But first, she won tournaments."

So that night Nancy stayed out of the disco. From her mo-tel room, she called her father to wish him an early happy Father's Day. The week before in Ohio, she had been so confi-dent that she had promised him the L.P.G.A. championship as his present. Now, she was thinking about a pool table as his official gift.

Sunday, the final round, was a little less damp at Locust Hill, but the tension was great. As much as Jane Blalock was respected, there was not a writer between Buffalo and Syracuse who didn't want Nancy Lopez to catch up and break the waiting records. Nancy wore a green-and-white striped skirt instead of the pants of the days before. As she walked to the practice green, someone gave her a five-leaf shamrock for good luck. There were girls wearing T-shirts with the New Mexico sun symbol. There was a young man in a football jersey that read "Drive for Five" above his number.

Stepping up to the first tee before a crowd about twice the size of the one the year before, she displayed a cool that might be the envy of basketball superstar Julius Erving: smiling broadly, tossing a little gloved wave, tipping her visor, then whacking a 270-yard drive down the fairway.

The game was close, all the way to the finish. By the 17th hole, she and Jane Blalock were still dead even. Nancy drew a deep breath and knocked in the most important shot she had ever made. For it gave her the lead.

Later, inside the pressroom she went directly to the phone, dialed New Mexico and shouted, "Dad, I won!" Her nose twitched and the tears came again. Her father was crying too. "I played really well today," she told him. "Happy Father's Day."

Nancy Lopez is bound to lose tournaments, but no one doubts she is a champion who can win over the long run. She will not be just a one-year hit. Meanwhile, her commercial career is under way. She has endorsed golf clubs and wrist watches and become the touring pro for a Florida resort.

Luckily, Nancy Lopez seems to be able to keep these things where they belong. On the golf course she remains all business, concentrating on her game.

She plainly adores playing golf. Hitting a solid drive, she says, is "like when you're really thirsty and you get a glass of iced tea. It feels so-o-o-o good!"

Yet in Nancy Lopez's mind, playing golf means something more. "I feel that's why I was put on this earth," she says. "I feel like I'm making people believe in a lot of things."

Perhaps the most inviting part of Nancy's personality is that she has not forgotten how far she has come. "I remember when I was an amateur watching professional tournaments, and how I idolized all those professional golfers. Sometimes when I'm playing, I'll look into the crowd. I just relate with the way it was when I was out there, behind the ropes."

Number of Words: 2752 ÷ _____ Minutes Reading Time = Rate _____

I. OUTLINING

Complete the following outline of the selection. Write the sentence from the following list where it belongs in the outline.

1. She is special on the golf course.
2. By her early teens, she had made a name for herself.
3. She has a go-for-it attitude.
4. She trailed him on the course.
5. She has a deadly putting game.

I. Nancy learned golf as a child.
   A. Her father gave her the only lessons she ever had.

      1. _____

      2. She learned with sawed-off clubs.

   B. _____

II. _____
   A. _____
   B. She is a charmer.
   C. _____

10 points for each correct answer   SCORE: _____

II. INFERENCES

Check √ five statements below which can be inferred from the story.

_____ 1. Nancy has attracted attention mostly because she is Mexican-American, which is rare among golfers.

_____ 2. Nancy's fast rise in the women's pro tour is unique and shows her unusual talents as a golfer.

_____ 3. Women's golf has gained as much from Nancy's success as she has gained from taking part in it.

_____ **4.** It is more difficult to be successful in the women's pro tour than in the men's.

_____ **5.** Because she has such a warm personality, Nancy is well-liked by the other women on the pro tour.

_____ **6.** To become as good as she is, Nancy has had to practice for many years.

_____ **7.** In spite of her success, Nancy has remained a nice, immediately likable person.

5 points for each correct answer   SCORE: _____

III. STORY ELEMENTS

Check √ *five methods which the author used to make readers like Nancy very much.*

_____ **1.** eye-witness report

_____ **2.** dialect

_____ **3.** newspaper article

_____ **4.** direct quotes

_____ **5.** biographical details

_____ **6.** feeling of mystery

_____ **7.** jokes and other humor

_____ **8.** describes events

5 points for each correct answer   SCORE: _____

PERFECT TOTAL SCORE: 100   TOTAL SCORE: _____

IV. QUESTIONS FOR THOUGHT

Do you have (or wish you had) a special skill or talent you would like to develop? How would you go about developing it?

Down a Dark Hall at Breakneck Speed

Sam Posey

The 24-hour race at Le Mans is a monument to the idea that life goes on. It is a French national institution more than half a century old, with a quarter-million fans turning out every June to watch it. But to the driver, speeding through the night portion of the race in a vehicle that is about as sturdy as an eggshell, with lights as useful at 200 miles per hour (320 kilometers per hour) as miner's lamps, the idea that life will go on—or that the night will ever end—doesn't seem the least bit assured.

At any time, day or night, Le Mans is a grand circuit. Its many fast turns allow laps of a very high average speed. But, because the track is narrow and lined with guardrails, the feeling is of aiming your car down a twisting hallway. A lap is about 8.5 miles (13.6 kilometers) long and takes you through the rural countryside on the outskirts of the railhead town of Le Mans, 115 miles (185 kilometers) southwest of Paris. Most of the circuit is made up of main roads usually open for public use. You rip past fields and farmhouses and plunge through dense pine forests. At racing speeds, however, you rarely notice the scenery.

At night there's almost nothing to see except the road. Cars are just twin dots of light. The few lighted landmarks surge at you out of the dark in an endless sequence that repeats itself. For the rest of the lap, rows of bright reflectors along both sides of the road outline the route clearly but make it look more like a lighted diagram than a race circuit. In this way, the night hides many dangers of the course.

Half of a Le Mans driver's night is spent on the track, the other half trying to get some sleep while his co-driver is out with the car. In the eight years I have done the race, I have always gone to my trailer knowing I must sleep to keep my reflexes working. But sleep has never been easy to come by. In the darkness I see images of the road rushing at me, as if all those laps have been stamped on my mind, a tape loop that cannot be shut off. If I close my eyes, a second later I'm grabbing for the edge of the cot, sure that I'm falling. When I am especially tired, I get the idea that my car is still going only because the whole team is willing it to run—sheer mind over matter. For me to sleep is to reduce by one the force that keeps us racing.

One year, 1970, I spent my hours in the trailer half-believing I would not live through the night. That was the year it rained for 20 of the 24 hours. Rain is frightening even on a slow track in broad daylight. At night, driving through Le Mans's fast turns and down the 4.5-mile (7.6 kilometer) straightaway to the town of Mulsanne, it was terrifying. On the water-soaked track, the tires of my Ferrari aquaplaned uncontrollably. The steering wheel was sometimes wrenched back and forth in my hands, and sometimes it went dead. Seen from the cockpit, the rain didn't fall; it came at me from the side.

Drivers usually remain at the wheel for three hours or more during the night, allowing their co-drivers a chance to rest. But in the rain that year, the needed concentration was so great that no one could stay on the track for more than 90 minutes at a stretch. I made so many trips back to the trailer, I lost count. Each time I took with me fresh memories of disaster, of fires burning around the track, wrecked cars, shiny slickers of rescue workers, a flag marshal dead, you name it.

In 1976 the Le Mans night was different. It was humid,

the air hanging heavy and close, promising another hot day. But it was clear—no chance of rain. I was driving for the BMW team, and, at 1 a.m. between stints at the wheel, I was lying on a cot in one of our trailers.

Unable to sleep, I thought back to the start of the race, which seemed a very long time ago. I remembered posing for pictures in front of the car, clowning with my co-drivers to take away the tension. And I remembered the first lap, racing down the Mulsanne straightaway, the cars weaving in and out. We all had energy to spare, then.

I got up and crossed the compound to the team camper. It was empty, its lights on. I poured some coffee. It

was almost time for my next turn at the wheel. You could be back home in California, I told myself, lying on the lawn, listening to the Pacific Ocean.

In the pit I ducked under the refueling hoses that hung from the low ceiling and pulled out my equipment bag. A minute later I was ready. The car came in, and co-driver Hughes de Fierlant shouted something to me that I couldn't hear. And then I was down in the cockpit of the car struggling with the harnesses. In a moment, I was moving up the pit lane. The lights of the grandstand were gone, and there was only the pool of my own lights ahead of me on the track.

The first lap was awkward as the new tires, cold and slip-

pery to begin with, slowly began to heat up. Then they were hot and sticky, and the car was gripping surely, as I thought it would. I drove in a groove that I had developed during my earlier shifts, guiding the car with the fewest possible movements. After six or seven laps, I felt the return of a strange sense: being in a giant orbit around a central point.

On my trips down the Mulsanne straight, I could feel the power releasing through the car as it picked up speed second by second. By a quarter of the way along, the car was in a snug envelope of air that tugged at its sides, making it dart from side to side like an express train on a rough roadbed.

Where there were other cars on the straight, I would duck into the vacuum behind them for a few seconds before passing. The maneuver both helped and hindered. In those moments, the view up the straight would be cut off. Full speed, and all I could see was 6 feet into the back of the car ahead. The Porsches had turbochargers: their exhausts glowed red with heat, and from under their wheels the passing lines painted on the road came spitting out like tracer bullets.

At other tracks you are still picking up speed when it comes time to brake at the end of the straight. But the Mulsanne is so long, the car comes to a stage where its power simply cannot push any more air out of its way, and the speed levels off. In the BMW this occurred at 185 miles per hour

(298 kilometers per hour). Surprisingly, instead of my feeling speed, the sensation was of being still, with the road, like a huge conveyor belt, rushing by below. The instruments glowed green in the dark. The guardrail reflectors streamed by like twin strings of bright pearls. I shifted a little in the seat, aware of my sweat-soaked suit. I felt warm, mellow and secure.

Three reflecting signs mark the approach of the Mulsanne kink, where the road dives to the right. It isn't so much a turn as a swerve; it can be taken flat out, but only with perfect timing. Just after the signs, the

road rises under the car as if the macadam has drawn a deep breath. This points the nose of the car up, and at that moment you must start the turn while your lights are pointed up into the trees beyond. You turn into the darkness, every lap requir-

ing the faith that you will do it at the right instant and that there will be no oil on the track.

The signs came up, then were gone behind me in the dark. I felt the road lift under the car and saw the lights point into the trees. An arch in the road started the steering wheel to the right. For one beat, my hands resisted the turning, then followed it through with a gentle wrist movement.

So it went, the night and the fatigue combining until, with no warning, a lap came where I knew something wasn't the same. Slowly I turned my head to the left. On the horizon, a long crayoned line of deep red signaled the dawn.

Within two laps I could see faint bits of light through the trees. Soon after that I could see the other drivers in their cars, shadows in cockpits, forces that, like me, had made it through the night. Of course, each was a threat now to my success in the race. But there was that moment of kinship, the cheery wave as I went by.

In the pits, when my turn was over, there were smiles all around. How's it going? Want some breakfast? It was good to talk to the reporters, who looked fresh after sleeping at their hotels. The stands were filling with people again.

Ten hours still stretched ahead before the finish. Repeatedly, we fought our way into top positions only to be delayed by nagging mechanical problems. My laps around the nearly empty track had a dreamlike quality, shaded always by the fear that, even at the last moment, something might go wrong and our whole effort would be nothing. To last through the night and then not last the race would be puzzling and unfair. The car just had to finish.

In the last laps, when the crowd was emptying over the guardrails onto the track, and the marshals were waving their flags like semaphores and the car felt strong under me, I knew we had it made. We had finished. In 24 hours we had gone 2565 miles (4127 kilometers), 299 times around the same 8-mile (13-kilometer) track. And we had come in tenth. Suddenly I realized I couldn't remember what the night had been like, couldn't remember at all.

Number of Words: 1747 ÷ _____ Minutes Reading Time = Rate _____

I. MAIN IDEA

Check ✓ *the one statement that best describes what the story is about.*

_____ **1.** Car racing is one of the most dangerous sports.

_____ **2.** Winning the Le Mans 24-hour race is every driver's dream.

_____ **3.** A driver describes how driving at Le Mans feels.

20 points for correct answer   SCORE: _____

II. LANGUAGE USAGE

When making comparisons, the author uses colorful language. Circle the letter of the sentence in each group that explains the phrase in italics.

1. The vehicle is about *as sturdy as an eggshell.*
    a. The car is strong and well built.
    b. The car is fragile and would break up in a crash.
    c. The car is very streamlined.
2. The headlights are *as useful at 200 mph as a miner's lamp.*
    a. The lights are not very helpful to the driver.
    b. The lights let the driver see quite well in the dark.
    c. The lights tend to blind the driver.
3. The train felt *like an express train on a rough roadbed.*
    a. The car felt bigger and heavier than it really was.
    b. The car was smooth and swift.
    c. The car seemed to be moving by itself over the bumpy road.
4. The passing lines came *spitting out like tracer bullets.*
    a. The outlines of the road clearly pointed the way ahead.
    b. The road appeared dangerously narrow.
    c. It looked as if the road was moving, and not the cars.

10 points for each correct answer   SCORE: _____

III. SUMMARY

Check √ two statements below that should be included in a short summary of the story.

_____ 1.   Le Mans is a very difficult, exhausting race for drivers.

_____ 2.   Only specially trained drivers can race at Le Mans.

_____ 3.   At night, drivers have to race their cars more slowly.

_____ 4.   Just finishing the 24-hour race is an achievement.

10 points for each correct answer   SCORE: _____

IV. CRITICAL THINKING

Decide whether each of the statements below is based on fact, or shows its writer's bias. Write F for fact and B for bias.

_____ 1.   At racing speeds, you scarcely notice the scenery.

_____ 2.   At night, many dangers of the racing track are hidden.

_____ 3.   Rain is dangerous even on a slow track in broad daylight.

_____ 4.   Not to finish a race is puzzling and unfair.

5 points for each correct answer   SCORE: _____

PERFECT TOTAL SCORE: 100   TOTAL SCORE: _____

V. QUESTIONS FOR THOUGHT

What do you imagine is the most attractive part of a Le Mans-style race? How would you prepare yourself for the race? Describe your feelings and ideas.

Exploring the Unexplained

Frank Edwards, David Wallachinsky
and Irving Wallace

The moment you see the place, something tells you that nature has gone mad. If you are on horseback, the horse will shy away from it. Birds suddenly swing about in flight and dart away. Even the trees give you the feeling that they, too, are moved by a power they cannot escape. For within a strange circle of crazy gravity, you can see the tree limbs droop. The trees themselves lean toward the magnetic north, although the trees around them point straight up.

This is the world-famed Oregon Vortex. It lies along the banks of Sardine Creek about 30 miles (48 kilometers) from Grant's Pass, Oregon. What the vortex does is well known, but why and how remain unanswered questions. This vortex does not seem to follow known scientific laws.

The vortex is about 165 feet (50 meters) in diameter. It is shaped roughly like a circle. But instruments show that the exact size of the troubled zone changes a bit from time to time—about every 90 days. Within this circle is an old wooden shed, once used as a place to test, weigh, and measure ores mined in the area. Back about 1890, when the scales began to play tricks, no one wanted to use the place. At the time, the shed was uphill, about 40 feet (12 meters) outside the limits of the vortex. After the shack was abandoned, that part of the hill slid down to its present place.

When you step inside the building, you're in another sort of world. You feel a huge pull downward, as if gravity had suddenly grown stronger. You lean naturally at about a 10-degree angle toward the center of the circle. If you lean toward the outside of the circle, you still get the creepy feeling of being pulled toward its center. And instruments show that you are!

Visitors are surprised when they see empty glass jars roll uphill. A handful of tiny paper scraps tossed into the air will spiral madly about as though stirred in midair by some unseen hand. It is a creepy feeling in an eerie setting.

If two people of equal height stand a short distance apart, one will seem to be taller than the other to anyone looking at the pair. According to a guide: "As another person goes away from you toward the south, he becomes taller. This is contrary to the laws of perspective, and must be seen to be believed." Is it merely a sight trick helped by a lively imagination?

Many scientists have done long experiments at the vortex, trying to solve its riddle. They hung a 28-pound (13-kilogram) steel ball on a chain from a beam in the old shack. Against

the laws of gravity, this ball dangles toward the center of the circle. You can easily push the ball toward the center of the circle. But it is harder to shove the ball toward the rim of the circle.

Among the massive pyramids of Giza is the Great Pyramid of Cheops in background.

Instruments have been used to measure the outer limits of the disturbance. The size of the circle is roughly 165 feet (50 meters). Other instruments were carefully set up outside the area of the vortex's pull. By looking through the planes of these devices, it was easy to say for sure that the feeling of standing at an angle within the circle was real.

By the same method, it was easy to prove that the 28-pound (12.78-kilogram) steel ball hanging from the chain inside the shack really does hang at an angle toward the center of the vortex. Golf clubs, brooms and other odds and ends of that general shape and length are easy to stand on end inside the freakish circle. In order to be balanced, they must be leaned at an angle away from the center of the vortex.

The vortex forces have an electromagnetic source. This has been proven by the way they act: an ordinary photographer's light meter, which changes light into electricity and shows it on a dial, will show wide differences between the daylight inside the circle and the daylight beyond the circle's limits. Compasses simply refuse to function.

There are other places where gravity acts differently in the United States, but none act as powerfully as the Oregon Vortex.

The force is there. It can be measured, but what it is and why it is nobody really knows. The Oregon Vortex is perhaps the "craziest" spot on earth, and it certainly ranks high among the oddest.

Another oddity is the mysterious Cheops Pyramid in Egypt. The stones in the pyramid built by Cheops about 2650 B.C. are put together so exactly you can't get a piece of paper between them. The pyramid itself weighs at least 6 million tons. Traditional history tells us that it was built during the 22 years of Cheops' reign by 4000 stone masons and 100,000 workers. Each year they spent three months dragging the stones into position.

The mystery? Some of the stones weigh as much as 5 tons. How could humans, working with simple machines, lift those stones? How were the 100,000 workers fed? How were the stone masons able to shape the stones so exactly?

What's inside the pyramid? The entrance to the "chamber

of the king," where Cheops was supposed to be buried, was plugged with a piece of granite larger than the corridor. The Arabs found it when they entered the tomb for the first time in the 9th century. Inside the tomb they found no body or tools, only a box of red granite. The mystery? The granite plug, because it was larger than the corridor, had to be placed there during the building. How could grave robbers get in, then? What was the box for?

In 1969 Dr. Walter Alvarez, a Nobel Prize-winner, led a group of American scientists in setting up cosmic-ray detectors around the tomb. He thought they could discover the location of the hidden chambers, since cosmic rays would pass through empty space more quickly than through solid stone. A strange thing happened—the readings for one day were not the same as the readings for another. Dr. Amr Gohed, who was in charge of

This bare granite box, empty today, once contained the mummy of the Pharoah.

the IBM 1130 computer center the research team used, said of the readings: "It defies all known laws of science and electronics. Either the geometry of the pyramid is in great error, which would affect our readings, or there is a mystery which cannot be explained. There is some influence that defies the laws of science at work in the pyramid."

Another mystery—why was the pyramid really built? Long, long ago, there were those who believed that the philosophers' stone, a power able to change base metal into gold, was hidden inside the pyramid.

The height of the pyramid is about 490 feet (148 meters), a measure directly related to the distance from the earth to the sun—about 92,096,451 miles (148,208,000 kilometers). (This distance was not figured so exactly until 1860 A.D.) The pyramid is lined up with the main points of the compass. There is an error of only 4°35'. The mystery? If the pyramid was built not as a tomb but as an astronomy tower, how were the Egyptians able to make such exact measurements?

All kinds of people—from archeologists to mystics—have theories about the pyramids.

Some people think the pyramid was a giant grain elevator, but there is not much proof to back up this theory.

How was it built? Some say that the stones were floated up the Nile on rafts, then put in place with wooden rollers. But, to float a 5-ton stone, a raft would have to displace 5 tons of water. There is no proof that the Egyptians had such monster rafts.

Others say that the pyramid was built by the great super race of Atlantis. Still others say it was built by beings from outer space.

Morris K. Jessup, astrophysicist and UFO buff, says, "Levitation is the only feasible answer. I believe that this lifting machine was a spaceship that brought colonists to various parts of the earth. It probably supplied the heavy lift power to build great stone works and was suddenly destroyed or taken away." Such an idea would support all the movements of stone that archeologists and engineers have thought about again and again.

If you prefer to examine mysteries closer and have given up trying to solve the Oregon Vortex mystery, there are always the moving coffins of Barbados, West Indies.

On a coral shelf 100 feet (30 meters) above sea level stands the beautiful cemetery of Christ Church, where people of wealth in Barbados put up family vaults. The vault of the Barbados coffins mystery is built partly above and partly below ground. The top part is made of large coral blocks cemented together. The roof is arched, and the walls slope inward a bit. It was built in 1742 for the body of Colonel Thomas Elliott. But he was buried at sea instead.

In July 1807 the first body, that of Mrs. Thomasina Goddard, was put on the highest shelf of the vault in a plain wooden coffin.

Then the Chase family entered the picture. On February 22, 1808, baby Mary Chase died. She was placed in a heavy metal coffin and sealed in the vault. That same year, her older sister, Dorcas, died, and her body was also taken to the vault.

It took two strong men to open the outside door. Inside, the only light came from burning torches. When the inner door to the vault was opened, the men shouted with fear.

Mary Chase's coffin was standing on its head in the corner opposite from where it had been put!

The mourners righted Mary Chase's coffin and put Dorcas down next to her sister. A month later, Colonel Chase died and was also buried in the vault.

Eight years later, another member of the Chase family died. By this time, the hinges of the vault had rusted. When two strong men opened the door, they stared in terror. Mrs. Goddard's coffin, as usual, was in its place, but the Chase's coffin littered the floor. Strange, because it weighed about 500 pounds (227 kilograms) and needed four men to move it.

A month later, a woman who was putting flowers on a grave heard a "loud cracking noise" and the "sound of someone moaning" in the vault. Her horse began foaming at the mouth in terror and later had to be treated by a veterinarian. The Sunday after, several horses securely tied outside the church broke away in fear and galloped down the hill to die in the sea.

The vault was getting a bad name. The next funeral, this time for Samuel Brewster, drew a large crowd of more

than 1000 people, some from Cuba and Haiti. During a wild storm, the lead coffin was carried to the vault by four men. There, the same bone-chilling scene awaited the mourners— coffins, standing on end, were thrown around inside.

At this point, the governor of the island, Lord Combermere, became involved. The next funeral was for Mrs. Thomasina Clarke, daughter of Thomasina Goddard, whose coffin had always remained on the shelf where it had been put. Combermere went to the funeral and inspected the vault. He sounded for an underground passage but there was none. He ordered the workmen to replace the upended coffins before bringing in the new one. Then he had the floor covered with fine sand and a new lock put on the door. Finally, the door was sealed with a coating of cement. Combermere and others stuck their signet rings in it while the cement was still wet, making marks that could not be removed.

On April 18, 1820, Combermere opened the vault for the last time. The cement on the door had not been touched. After masons broke through it, they could not open the door more than half an inch because something was leaning against it. When they forced the door open, a heavy object fell down the inside steps with a crash— it was a coffin, of course. As they entered the vault, the masons saw a bony arm, that of Dorcas Chase, sticking out through a hole in the side of the coffin. All the other coffins, including Mrs. Goddard's, were scattered around the vault in complete disorder. Combermere gave up. He had the dead removed elsewhere for burial.

What do scientists have to say about these strange events? Researchers from the London Science Museum and the Society of Psychical Research studied the mystery of the Barbados coffins, but they came up with no answers.

It seems unlikely that the coffins were disturbed by earth movements because the vault was on a bed of coral. There was no underground passage and no entry to the vault except through the front door. In the final sealing of the vault, Governor Combermere had removed any possibility that someone had entered the vault secretly. Jewelry placed in the vault was not touched, so it is unlikely that the coffins were being disturbed by grave robbers. Nevertheless, the Elliott vault was no longer used as a final resting place for the Barbados dead.

Some of the most thrilling mysteries in the world are natural. If you like challenges, some of the biggest, strange-but-true mysteries are still waiting to be solved. For, unlike mystery stories in books and movies, none of these can be explained in the usual, scientific way. Yet all of these are recorded examples of something that does not seem to follow known scientific laws. These mysteries also show that there is much left to discover about the very real and natural forces at work around us.

Number of Words: 2303 ÷ _____ Minutes Reading Time = Rate _____

I. SKIMMING

Skim the text and find the information you need to match each place below (column A) with its description (column B).

	A		B
____	1. Chase family vault	a.	shaped roughly in a circle
____	2. Oregon Vortex	b.	in Egypt
____	3. Cheops Pyramid	c.	made of large coral blocks
		d.	totally below ground
		e.	by the Sardine creek

5 points for each correct answer   SCORE: _____

II. FACT/OPINION

Write F next to each sentence that is fact. Write O for each sentence that is opinion.

____ 1. Inside the Oregon Vortex, tree limbs droop, jars roll uphill, and objects lean towards the center of the circle.

____ 2. The Oregon Vortex gives you the creepy feeling of being moved by a power you cannot escape.

____ 3. The Cheops Pyramid could only have been built by using levitation, with the lifting force that came from a spaceship.

____ 4. The results of some experiments conducted at the Cheops Pyramid defy the known laws of science and electronics.

____ 5. In the Chase family vault, the coffins had moved, and were scattered in complete disorder.

5 points for each correct answer   SCORE: _____

III. GENERALIZATIONS

What does this story say about unexplained phenomena? Check √ four statements below that are generally true.

_____ 1. The world is full of mysterious places and events.

_____ 2. Certain facts or events cannot be explained logically.

_____ 3. Mysteries like the Vortex seem to defy natural laws.

_____ 4. Science is not advanced enough to explain these occurrences.

_____ 5. Unexplained phenomena prove that there are other intelligent creatures in the Universe.

10 points for each correct answer   SCORE: _____

IV. REFERENCE

In a book on strange phenomena where would you find the following information? Write the letter of the answer in the space below:

a. the subjects alphabetized   **c.** date of publication
b. chapter titles   **d.** additional information
                                                          about text

_____ 1. copyright   _____ 3. footnotes
_____ 2. table of contents   _____ 4. index

5 points for each correct answer   SCORE: _____

PERFECT TOTAL SCORE: 100   TOTAL SCORE: _____

V. QUESTIONS FOR THOUGHT

What explanation do you have for any of the mysteries in this selection? Is there another natural mystery which you know about that wasn't covered in this selection?